Temperatism, Volume I

Temperatism, Volume I

A New Way to Think About Business and Doing Good

Carrie Foster

BEP BUSINESS EXPERT PRESS

Temperatism, Volume I: A New Way to Think about Business and Doing Good
Copyright © Business Expert Press, LLC, 2018.

First published in 2018 by
Business Expert Press, LLC
222 East 46th Street, New York, NY 10017
www.businessexpertpress.com

ISBN-13: 978-1-63157-772-7 (paperback)
ISBN-13: 978-1-63157-773-4 (e-book)

Business Expert Press Human Resource Management and Organizational Behavior Collection

Collection ISSN: 1946-5637 (print)
Collection ISSN: 1946-5645 (electronic)

Cover and interior design by S4Carlisle Publishing Services Private Ltd., Chennai, India

First edition: 2018

10 9 8 7 6 5 4 3 2 1

Printed in the United States of America.

Abstract

This book isn't intended to have all the answers, but explores the question 'How much wealth is enough?' Examining the idea that the capitalist profit agenda is not benefiting society or democracy, *Temperatism* investigates whether there is an alternative to the profit agenda currently followed by organizations and society. If growth and profit are an important part of the equation, then the question that arises is "Important for what purpose?" What follows is a proposition of an alternative agenda of doing good and the introduction of a new business framework—temperatism.

Keywords

Legacy, organization studies, people and purpose before profit, talent potential

Contents

Preface

If at first the idea is not absurd, then there is no hope for it.

—Albert Einstein

Questions are my stock and trade when coaching executives or working as an organization development practitioner. "What if" questions are great for driving innovation and creativity and for jumping people out of their normal linear thinking and getting them to take a look at things from a different angle, opening up their mind to new ideas, absurd ideas, ridiculous notions that might, just might, be the answer and solution we were looking for all along.

In 2011, I was listening to a news broadcast and there was a feature on the Mountain of Mammon, referring to the continuous pursuit of wealth at all costs. At the time, it caught something in me and I wrote a blog pondering the question *"What if organizations pursued something other than an economic agenda?"* Now, as I write this in early 2017, I find the same references to the Mountain of Mammon appearing on the news. The continuing failure of the free market to stagnating wages has changed the world from neoliberal stability where globalism was seen as inevitable to one where populism is threatening the established order of Western democracies. Perhaps, today, this childlike innocent question is more pertinent than ever before.

The question is perhaps searching for a more constructive solution versus the populist reaction to the failings of the capitalist economic system that has seen the gap between rich and poor widen and globalism cause whole sections of society to be put out of work as jobs move abroad. As a gig worker I am part of the capitalist system, selling my services where there is demand, taking me across the UK, Europe, and the Middle East. In my organization development practice and as a lecturer on business courses I have encountered many executives and business leaders who believe quite passionately that economic forces should focus on profit and wealth creation and "everything else" such as poverty, inequality, health, wellbeing, environmental, ethical, and sustainability issues will magically solve themselves because of the "trickle-down effect." Inequality is celebrated in capitalism since "efforts to create a more equal society are both counterproductive and morally corrosive. The market ensures that everyone gets what they deserve" (Montboit, 2016). Andrew Carnegie (1906) in his book *The Gospel of Wealth* argues that only capitalism is capable of creating positive economic conditions in which society can create wealth. He goes on to propose that the wealthy few is an inevitable consequence of capitalism, but it is beholden to those who possess great wealth to live modestly and help those less fortunate. I hear how society benefits from successful capitalists but can't help wondering whether the inevitability of capitalism was true and that "this" was really all we could expect from our economic system: greed, self-interest, and crumbs from the table.

I say this as someone who enjoys the fruits of my labor, but who has also experienced a period in which, by Western standards, my family existed in poverty. We lived on the verge of losing it all, struggling to pay bills, wondering how to feed the kids, and my husband and I having to miss meals. Despite this, I was still able to work on an expensive laptop in a centrally heated house, listening to music on my iPod, while my children attended school. Even when we had tipped from just about managing to not managing by modern standards, we were still in the top 6 to 10 percent of wealthy in the world. So I guess the question that confronts me is "*How much wealth is enough?*"

I don't believe it is wrong to have nice things. Material things do make our lives easier and more enjoyable. Nor do I think profit is a necessarily evil. But there are undeniable issues of proportionality, equality, effort, reward, responsibility, and basic human needs that should be considered. With climate change firmly on the agenda despite the denier's best efforts, we can no longer ignore questions about who ends up bearing the consequences of the external costs of our activities. Growth and profit are an important part of the equation, but they should not be the answer; therefore, this leaves us with the question of "*Important for what purpose?*"

It cannot be claimed that the ideas explored in this book are any more new or different from the ideas expressed by many other writers both historically and in the present time. But my intention is to offer an alternative, positive approach to change, which perhaps contrasts with the current climate of angry destruction, opposition, and divisiveness. Rather than dismantling everything and reverting to tribalism I believe that there is a way we can together, as the human race, move toward a positive change, a change for good.

My interest in contributing to the debate on how to change the system comes from a simple desire to help every individual release their talent potential. I believe passionately that with the right environment and circumstances, people's potential can be released not only for the benefit of the individual but for the benefit of the society at large. "Amartya Sen the economist-philosopher and Nobel Prize Laureate, [said] that poverty leads to an intolerable waste of talent. As he puts it, poverty is not just a lack of money; it is not having the capability to realize one's full potential as a human being" (Banerjee and Duflo, 2012). My experience of developing people has led me to believe that we are all born for a purpose, everyone has something valuable to contribute, and any actions or circumstances that prevent individuals from being all that they are meant to be causes an incalculable loss. I also believe in the potential of the human race, that between us, we have the knowledge, skills, and capability to make the changes that are needed to achieve a better world for everyone.

This book isn't intended to have all the answers, but to get you thinking about the idea that the capitalist profit agenda does not have to be the only agenda that organizations and society have to follow. Given today's climate I don't think suggesting a replacement for capitalism is perhaps as radical as it was even five years ago. Indeed Mason (2016) recently offered the term *post-capitalism* to explain the need for a strategic shift for both neoliberalism and capitalism. I offer a different perspective while recognizing the same problems. My approach stems from a desire for a more human approach to solving a global problem and a commitment to releasing talent potential for everyone. I can't help feeling that there is a certain rightness to the idea that humans are socially conscious, deserve, and want better than being enslaved materialistic consumers and that the inequality of wealth in the world isn't only unsustainable but also inevitable. I propose that rather than racing toward mutual destruction, nationalism, and deeper levels of selfishness, there is an alternative agenda of doing good, which sits under a framework I've labeled *Temperatism*.

So I ask, as you read through this book, you consider my proposals in the context of our world, which is on the edge of chaos, but with an eye on the equal worth of every individual in it. Be sure that as you read this, you are part of something bigger. You can #bethechange for no other reason than because you are part of the most amazing, inventive, innovative, and creative species on earth, the human race. And I believe that together we can change for good.

Best wishes
Carrie Foster

Acknowledgment

I would like to thank my friends and family who have allowed me the room to explore and search for meaning in too many books, articles, and journals, trying to make sense of the ideas in my head and the desire for the world to be a better version than it is today. I would like to thank BEP for giving me the opportunity to write what I am passionate about and for providing me with a platform from which I can share these ideas with others.

CHAPTER 1

Introduction

We must overcome the notion that we must be regular . . . it robs you
of the chance to be extraordinary and leads you to the mediocre.
—Uta Hagen

2016 was a year of seismic change. It wasn't just the deaths of many
well-known celebrities that had filled Facebook streams. The online
debates and media recoiled through a range of issues such as the migrant crisis, Brexit, ISIS, Russia, Kim Jong-un's missiles, and Trump. For
years neo-liberal stability had dulled the populace into a secure blanket
of apathy and disengagement with political processes. This was the way
things were done, and there wasn't any way in which the ordinary folk
could change things. Fastforward to today and a seismic shift has taken
place. Whether it is worldwide protests, political rallies, or the swell of
populism, what has been and what will be is a vibrant battle-ground of
competing ideas and interests. The current instability in the world has
reignited debate about how the world should be run and questions about
the validity of the world order. People are searching for a new way of
doing things. I'm not sure many people are necessarily looking for a new
ideology, but there is a growing demand for us to separate ourselves from
what had been an accepted norm in the way that humanity conducts itself
on planet Earth.

Since the 2008 credit crunch, the world seemed to have entered a
permanent state of gloom and depression. There is a dearth of worries
consuming individuals and institutions: climate change, austerity, terror-
ism, and globalization. Sovereign nations are no closer to fighting off the
scourge of sovereign debt, and despite evidence of greater levels of material wealth and prosperity still being present, the backlash is a result of

increased levels of introspection in regard to the social failings that our current system has created. As the leaders of Western liberal democracies examine the popular uprising and increasing criticism of the systems failings, they are faced with questions about what decisions blew them off course and whether they might have actually been, whisper it, wrong.

Occasionally humanity comes to a crossroads where a new generation of thinkers and writers rise up and begin to question the way the world is organized. These thinkers are no more qualified than your average Joe to bring words of wisdom to the masses. But they are passionate and they believe enough in what they think the society is thinking to stick their heads above the parapet and stand up to be counted. As the world population exceeds the 7.5 billion mark, our voices can easily be lost in the cacophony of sound, especially in a world that has embraced mass communication, enabled by the digital age. The constraints we face are not in our ability to think, nor in our ability to communicate what we think, but rather in our ability to be heard above the noise. To call out in a way that makes society sit up and take notice. To make people care enough to convert the call to arms into action.

In writing this book, it is hoped that the ideas expressed within will seed a movement that the expression of the #changeforgood idea will catch hold and spread like a modern day pandemic. It is hoped that the ideas will reach the ears and hearts of those who are willing to take a stand, and they will join together to demand the world takes notice and makes a shift that puts people first. There is some urgency, to this mission, we cannot and must not delay, "severe resource constraints and dramatically shifting demographics means significant challenges ahead" (CIPD, 2012). We don't have time to remain idle and pretend that these things don't matter anymore. Ashford, writing in 2010, stated that "in approximate terms 1% of the population owns 50% of the capital wealth and 10% own 90%. That leaves the remaining 90%, who own little or no capital (half of whom have a negative net worth), with little or no time for thoughtful politics as they scramble for the 10% of wealth that is left." Today, less than a decade later, the shift in these figures provide a sobering reality check on the rapid growth of inequality in our world. A report by Oxfam in 2016 offered these startling facts:

- 62 people own as much as the poorest half of the world's population
- In 2015, the 1 percent owned more than the 99 percent
- The wealth of the world's poorest population had fallen by 38 percent since 2010

(Oxfam, 2016)

If the world is going to avoid a total system failure, catastrophic levels of social unrest, and a chaotic and possibly war-ridden retreat from globalization, change must happen. The question is whether that change can be a good change and whether the change will be for good, preventing us from returning to the way things are today.

CHAPTER 2

Why Now? Why Temperatism?

This is the question I want everyone to ask yourself every single day when you come with something you feel that needs to be done: if not now, then when? And if not me, then who?

—Mick Ebeling

Historically, it seems that in many cases the -ism's and -ology's occurred first as a conversation in coffee shops, before eventually becoming formalized in the written word to be debated and discussed by a wider audience. But previous ideologies were restricted to the philosophers, the academics, and those who were classed as the thinkers of the day. Today, the forum for debate is wider, the opportunity to contribute to thinking no longer restricted to the "thinking classes" but to anyone who can think. Temperatism might be an idea that, for the first time in human social history, can be debated, formed, and built upon using the shared values and beliefs of anyone, anywhere. Social media, the World Wide Web, and global communication offer the opportunity for anyone who is interested to join the debate.

Sometimes the theories and concepts explored by writers touch an understanding that makes people stand up and listen. They verbalize what people are feeling and connect an intellectual understanding to create a powerful mix that can change cultures, improve society, and affect the world. This book is being written in response to ideas that are readily available to anyone who cares to research them. The opinions and ideas expressed are as a direct result of watching news programs, interacting on social media, working in organizations, and having a personal curiosity of social humanist thinking. It is also being written as a result of frustration as to why humanity refuses to change course despite the mounting evidence that we are heading for the edge of a perilous cliff that could end our very existence.

The global recession caused by the 2008 credit crunch and continuing sovereign debt issues provide, perhaps, the greatest opportunity for a discussion into the appropriateness of Western capitalism as a global model of human interaction and its associations with democratic values and individual freedom. "We are thus sitting on the ruins of several failed paradigms: the real socialism, the reformed golden age capitalism, the neo-liberal market fundamentalism, the Washington consensus and last but not least, social democracy. Paradoxically, one may draw a positive conclusion from this dismal situation: we are condemned to invent new paradigms for the twenty-first century" (Sachs, 2009). Today, we can look back on a decade of hedonistic pursuit of year-on-year growth enabled by perverse levels of individual, corporate, and government debt, the demise of socialist and communist economic and political systems, and the rise of the knowledge economy and find ourselves in a world that is suffering from a capitalist hangover of global proportions.

Politicians and the public are demanding that the global economy be up and running, that recovery should be happening now, and the fact that it isn't, a decade after the crunch, is a frustration. The issue now, of course, is not that the economy isn't doing well at creating wealth; it's just the economy is not doing well at creating wealth for most of the world's population. There are plenty of symptoms that all is not well—high living costs, wage stagnation, austerity programs, levels of sovereign and personal debt, etc.—but no one seems willing to pinpoint what the real illness is. We all know that the Western economies are ill, but they are all avoiding the obvious in regard to where to start to make it better.

The gross malfeasance of the banking sector, which led to the 2008 credit crunch, is not surprising when weighing the balance of power, regulation, and the pursuit of growth. Finance, which became so critical to the running of our economic system and has an important role socially, was transformed into a dangerous vehicle driven by fortune, greed, and competition. The circumstances of the recession were made worse by the penetration of financial influence into the realms of political power. Banking powerhouses were wooed by politicians and despite the bank's aggressive pursuit of personal enrichment were protected from their excesses and yet continue to fail to serve a useful purpose in regard to social contribution. The tragedy of our age is that the players in this game continue to have political influence and exert undue pressure to be allowed to continue their aggressive pursuit of profit and growth, without fear of the consequences and refusing to engage with their critics. There is no debate, only capitalism.

In a world where we expect things to be ready in an instant, it is impossible to galvanize a popular movement when you can't offer a quick fix to our problems. Politicians are under pressure, because there is an expectation that things should be fixed, more should be done, waiting for recovery is not acceptable. At the same time, the same people who are calling for more also believe that small government and free enterprise is the answer to the economic problems we are facing.

When it comes to electoral cycles and the media coverage of political opponents blaming each other because the promised change hasn't happened, the public has very often been placed into a position where they are forced to take a back seat driver position. The electorate, unhappy that change hadn't happened fast enough, doesn't seem to accept the fact that such deep-rooted problems, which have been decades in the making, are unlikely to have been turned around in a few years. In between elections, politicians tinker around the edges rather than tackling the systemic issues, which are causing the problems in the first place. The opposition and the public complain that the government, which has been in power only for a brief period of time, isn't "doing enough" to fix things. The problem is that "giving it time" and taking a root cause approach to change doesn't make a great sound bite for politicians dealing with a nation that is suffering now and wants things fixed.

Trump's pledge to Make America Great Again appeals to the needs of the forgotten majority who are exasperated with broken political pledges and what they feel is a broken system. The problem is the solutions offered: build the wall, throw out immigrants, drain the swamp, actually don't tackle the real problem. The ideological root upon which the system is built is capitalism.

The truth is that capitalism has made us all expect things to happen quickly. Short termism is at the center of our culture. It is extremely difficult to convince people that they should delay fulfilling what they want now, to not indulge for the sake of the long term or even for the sake of others. We want things to be right, right now. The 2008 recession is the worst since the Great Depression of the 1920s. It took 15 years for the world economy to recover from the trading excesses that contributed to the Great Depression. The recession we find ourselves in now is a result of the introduction of new rules that saved capitalism but resulted from New Deal rules designed to stop excess, being redacted. The credit crunch was almost a decade ago and yet we are expecting our governments to have sorted out the mess already. It is not realistic to expect politicians (who were elected after the problems started) to have all the answers and be able to do things that will have an immediate impact. The seeds of the recession were actually planted almost 40 years ago, when Reagan and Thatcher pursued a policy of muscular entrepreneurialism: "massive tax cuts for the rich, the crushing of unions, deregulation, privatization, outsourcing and competition in public services" (Monboit, 2016). This in turn led to the increasing financialization of the Western economies. The City and Wall Street have replaced the nonfinancial industrial and business sectors as the main power players in our society. Political parties and society seem incapable or unwilling to tackle or reform a system that is challenging the very rules of democratic citizenship.

Furthermore, consumers have got used to instant gratification, hence why there have been increasing levels of household debts. We no longer save up for something but rather operate on a *see it, want it, buy it* process because the new generation does not have the patience to wait to give things time to work themselves through the system. We want results and we want them now. The problem is that instant gratification is addictive. It is not because we don't *want* to wait; it is that we *can't* wait because the world we live in moves too fast. There is little to recommend in the way of a cure for short-term gratification that doesn't come with an end point that reads along the lines of "stop it." But sometimes change is as simple as that. Simply indulging in our base interests and allowing us to be ruled by peer pressure to act with civility can cure many of life's social ills.

Patience, of course, teaches us the value of delaying gratification, a skill necessary for maturity. Patience can help develop the ability to think through and resolve problems; it counteracts impulsivity and builds self-esteem, helping individuals hold themselves together in the face of difficulties. The value of patience lies in its ability to lead to inner calm and emotional strength of character. Patience helps us learn resilience, fortitude, self-containment, and the ability to avoid self-destructive behaviors. These are qualities needed for emotional maturity and sustainable performance. But patience relies on something more meaningful than simply waiting. It relies on us being in relationship with others, considering the needs of others as well as our own, and corporately changing the behavioral norms that will be necessary for the success of doing good in society. The problem is, of course, even as inhuman treatment and hateful behavior is tackled, it doesn't disappear; instead it exists in the shadows and then every now and again reemerging to remind us that we are not all that civil or good after all. While huge portions of the human race are exposed to high levels of deprivation and horror, for many of us our lives are dominated by first world problems. It is no good expecting separate individuals in society to deny instant gratification, if their neighbors, friends, family, colleagues, and peers are all indulging in self-gratification. Change will not happen if it is done individually. AA meetings have demonstrated the power of peer pressure in maintaining a change of behavior even for those in the grip of addiction. "Few major societal ills, in fact, are immune. Since our peers shape so much of our behavior, so much of it can be changed with peer pressure. This includes the pieces of what we do that then affect those around us. Peer pressure changes you and in turn you change a community, a bureaucracy, a culture, a government—a world" (Rosenburg, 2011).

Patience is also necessary in organizations where projects are expected to deliver results immediately—quick wins are important for any project or intervention that is delivered. But often the real prize may take months if not years to appear. But if the project doesn't deliver in this financial reporting quarter, it is deemed to have failed. In organizational and governmental life, old projects are rejected before they are embedded and new projects are started. In truth we no longer know which projects are delivering what results because we don't wait around long enough to let success show itself. When success comes, we can no longer be sure what has delivered the success because we have started and rejected so many projects in the time between "then" and "now" that there is no clear path to demonstrate cause and effect.

The current focus of organizations and governments and the capitalist system is the result of what Douglas Holmes refers to as "Fast Capitalism" (Holmes, 2002). The pursuit of short-term goals and the market reaction to quarterly results have replaced long-term measures that benefit people, the organization, and society as a whole. Investing in skills and developing people's potential is ignored because people become little more than arms, legs, and body that have tasks to do, a number on a spreadsheet that can be slashed with a tap on the keyboard. The pursuit of quick profit means that fast return on investment is demanded, but the delivery of short-term goals means no resource is given to projects that add value in the long term, and the end result is profit returns today are made at the expense of long-term prosperity.

The fundamental issue to these systemic pains is that currently no alternative argument or any reason exists for capitalism to stop, since the accumulation of wealth and acquisition of material goods has no end. There isn't an argument to finish what has been started when the global agenda and political, social, and economic arguments remain centered on profit and self-interest. In a world where "if it's good enough for me, it's good enough" is the central tenet of our existence, there is no need for a new ideology, or for us to seek out change. However, "the unbalanced structure of economic growth over the last decade has fed straight through to a disastrous social geography, bypassing the least advantaged in ways that they have done nothing to deserve while indiscriminately rewarding the wealthy" (Hutton, 2011). The problems that we are experiencing in the world, economically, socially, and politically, are a direct result of our pursuit of a finance-centric society that began with the foundations of a free-market economy laid during the Reagan and Thatcher years. What has emerged since then is "the exponential growth of the financial services industry," which has not only "created a financial-driven business environment," but also impacted our political, economic, and social culture to focus and be "dominated by its financial purpose to generate money and purely financial value" (CIPD, 2012).

The very dynamism and adaptability of the capitalist system makes it a slippery eel that relies on its beneficiaries destroying and discrediting any attempts to promote social change and an end to consumerism. However, there is a moral and human argument that the continual pursuit of profit and growth regardless of the way in which they are achieved is no longer sustainable. "Moreover, 'degrowth' is not a solution as long as poverty and exclusion remain pervasive. A redistribution of income and wealth is practically impossible in the absence of growth. Even those who rightly advocate as a paramount goal of development a 'civilization of being' recognize as a precondition the equitable 'sharing and having', a situation which is far from being achieved" (Sachs, 2009). Ryan Avent suggests that mass digital prosperity, which involves "redistributing resources from the people, firms and countries that are able to capture a large share of gains from to those that are not . . . will require social consensus that redistribution is both necessary and just" (CIPD, 2017). It would seem that the 99 percent that the Occupy movement suggested they represented are now determined to make their voices heard and demand that their value be fully accounted for and rewarded. Whether the current populist movement in Western society, which is demanding change, can grapple the power from the hands of the few into the service of the many is yet to be seen.

A New Ideology

It is within this context of instability and destructive demand for change that I seek to propose a new ideology, Temperatism, offering an exposition of a set of ideas based on a socio-humanist value system. In presenting these ideas, values, and beliefs as a manifesto of change based on the Temperatist ideology, there is a second purpose, to provoke a debate regarding the political, economic, and social systems, which govern our lives.

For much of the last century the ideological debate centered on socialist and capitalist ideologies. It has been argued that "capitalism has now broken every wall of resistance, penetrating societies and nations as never before imagined. Even nations like India and China which were once time sworn enemies of the pure capitalist system have finally succumbed to the political ideology of capitalism" (Ukpere and Slabbert, 2008). At the end of the first millennium, Blair offered the UK a "third way," which turned out not to be a third way at all, but a sacrificing of socialist ideals to win power in a market-dominated system. "Social democracy was reduced to a husk. Public action—like education and training—could be attempted only if the markets welcomed it. There could be no sustained expression of public purpose, social justice or reform of economic institutions if this went against the prevailing orthodoxy" (Hutton, 2011). In truth we live in a state where entrepreneurialism and piratical corporatism is the only socially acceptable condition, even for those with socialist values. You can say that you believe in fairness, but there is no mechanism left in order to fight for greater equality and putting social good first. For a long time and even more so now, any criticism of capitalism has been denounced as an attack on individual and the true reality of the negative aspects of the capitalist ideology are "intentionally obscured by the dominant parties," namely, commercial organizations and Western governments (Nienhueser, 2011). Monboit (2016) argues that neoliberalism offers freedom not for the man who needs protecting but from the strong in society; "freedom from trade unions and collective bargaining means the freedom to suppress wages. Freedom from regulation means the freedom to poison rivers, endanger workers, charge iniquitous rates of interest and design exotic financial instruments. Freedom from tax means freedom from the distribution of wealth that lifts people out of poverty." No matter how many recessions and crashes society is subjected to, capitalism bounces back, promising a way out of our woe, promising abundance and good times ahead and so the relentless pursuit of profit and competitive advantage continues unchecked, unashamed, and unabated. The theory and the eloquence of the free market are what have contributed to the current recession. The many imperfections of the system are ignored, as capitalism remains protected from its excesses by the political and economic elite. Too many of the costs that are incurred by society are dismissed by organizations in the accounting of their operations, and short-termism dominates the thinking of those who are in a position to make changes for the long term.

Dan Mayer (2007), in his paper "Corporate Citizenship and Trustworthy Capitalism: Co-creating a More Peaceful Planet," outlines five "mistaken mental frameworks" that our society has accepted as universal truths:

- "Corporations do not make war—governments do;
- Corporations are effectively governed or restrained from antisocial actions by the public sector and are subject to rules of the game set by public authority;

- America stands as a beacon of liberty and democracy, a peaceful republic that promotes freedom and free trade as a way to bring other nations into the fold of peaceful, trading nations;
- American free enterprise and corporate governance are the best available models of corporate efficiency and optimization of human and natural resources; and
- The modern corporation maintains a social contract with societies in which they operate, providing jobs, products and progress" (Mayer, 2007).

Although Mayer is commenting specifically on America, the mental models apply to Western capitalism and the pursuit of wealth creation through "free" trade. Capitalism has embarked upon decades of irrationality, where the maximization of profit today replaces the concerns for the future. There are organizations that do pursue a more socially and environmentally friendly purpose, but these are in the minority and are compromised by participation in a system that punishes the lack of quick profits. Most organizations and institutions are impacting the world negatively and at greater degrees as time moves on. However, because of the cultural beliefs of Western democracies, anything that challenges, or differs from the mental framework that Mayer outlines, is attacked vigorously. Temperatism does not propose that we begin to pursue an antibusiness course of action; rather it seeks to challenge the accepted mental model regarding the very role of organizations in society. It places under the microscope the pursuit of the profit agenda and seeks to replace self-interested short-termism with a doing good framework and organizations that purposefully seek to make a positive impact on the society and wider environment in which they operate.

The furious backlash to Obamacare in the United States is one recent example of how ideological propositions that go against capitalist thinking are blatantly described in emotional language of gross infringement of individual rights and government wrongdoing. Republicans, seeking to repeal and replace Obama's Healthcare Law, have described the current law as a "Ponzi scheme that would make Bernie Madoff proud," a "job killer" that "puts the federal government between you and your doctor" (Guardian, 2012).

The reason for proposing Temperatism now is that I believe that the core of what makes us human has been twisted out of all recognition and is under attack. Values and attributes that are core to what makes us human, including kindness, respect for others, inbuilt liberalism and democracy, social consciousness, and a sense of meaning and purposefulness to our lives, are being weakened, to the point that to demonstrate such values is met with suspicion and derision. There exists a backdrop of vacuous opposition to anything that does not align itself with the market-led capitalist ideology. This book and the ideas, beliefs, and values outlined offer a forum for sides to be formed. There will be those who disagree with the proposed Temperatist ideology and those who support it. Whatever side of the fence you fall, and the hope is that you *will* fall off the fence, as long as you are debating the world in which we live, then you become part of something bigger.

CHAPTER 3

Where Are We Now?

Until we address the profound economic and political disenchantment that led millions of voters to put their faith in the mendacious claims of a ragbag group of political malcontents, populists and opportunists, it will be difficult for our country to dream of a common future again.
—Nick Clegg

In Western society it is often argued that capitalism frees people from the shackles of the state, enabling them to claim ownership of the means of production and have freedom in their choice of activities, primarily who they choose to sell their labor to (Meltzer, 2012). Feudalism and colonialism were the preserve of the rich and powerful, but capitalism placed the power of economic advantage and advancement into the hands of the merchant classes. It allowed anyone to move up the ranks in society, to not be held back as a consequence of their birth, but instead have the freedom to achieve what they believed and made possible for themselves.

Indeed the architect of capitalism and free-market economic thinking, Adam Smith argued in his book *Wealth of Nations* that self-interest was the central theme: "It is not from the benevolence of the butcher, the brewer, or the baker, that we expect our dinner, but from their regard to their own interest. We address ourselves, not to their humanity but to their self-love and never talk to them of our own necessities but of their advantages" (CQ Research, 2010).

The Pursuit of Ownership

Sometimes it feels like we have all become obsessed with money and the acquisition mentality appears to drive our day-to-day behavior. Regardless of our economic position, the addiction to acquisition has gripped us all, to a point where we measure our own worth not by who we are, but by what material goods we have. But we now find ourselves, like all addicts do, in an ever-tightening grip of dependence. We sell our labor for money in order to acquire material things that require us to have more money to maintain or keep them safe. Our addiction has become terminal as the life span of our acquisitions is getting shorter and as the market focus on growth requires organizations to continue producing the latest, greatest must-haves. In this cycle of dependency on money and addiction to acquisition, the politicians beg big business and consumers to continue in the very behavior that was the cause of our current economic woe in the hope that it will somehow be our savior. Is it wrong to expect our politicians and corporations to begin to question their unwavering belief in the capitalist system? Should we not demand that we reconsider the absurdity of doing the same things but somehow expecting that we will get different results next time? Is it time for society to innovate and create rather than recycle and make do and mend a system that is broken and leads to brokenness? Is it possible to manage an orderly adaptation of the system, rather than succumb to the isolationist and protectionist agenda as advocated by the populist movement?

Our addiction to acquisition has, it seems, been fueled by the promotion of self-interest, which hooks into liberal ideas that emphasize key cultural values and democratic principles. We believe we have a right to indulge our every desire, because capitalism has hijacked values, such as those pertaining to individual rights, freedom, and autonomy to make choices, personal justice, and a noncoercive relationship between state, society, and the individual. But what is missing from capitalist values is the context of universality in securing these political and social freedoms. The equality demanded by the application of liberalism prevents capitalism from truly adopting pure liberal values because of its permissiveness and acceptance of inequality in wealth distribution. The schizophrenic adoption of both liberal and illiberal principles is driven primarily by capitalism's focus on property before people, individual wealth before societal good, and self before others. The attempt by the West to adopt neoliberal values was developed as a crisis-management response to the contradictions inherent in the capitalist system. The increasing dominance of financial services in the world market and the political will behind *laissez-faire* rules lulled consumers into a false sense of security regarding their rights and freedom. Capitalism promoted wealth creation as being based on a false promise of a benign global market, which promised to make us all richer on the basis of rational self-interestedness.

And yet for all this freedom, are workers happier today? We have got ourselves into a cycle of debt, consumerism, and misery. The self-destruction thesis argues that the very nature of capitalism's ethical compass driving self-interest results in its own ethics and processes being undermined. The processes involved in pursuing an agenda of self-interest destroy the ability of individuals to attain the goals that they are interested in and damage the sustainability of capitalism itself. For example, the executive who works 100 hours a week does so with a dream of one day being able to give it all up and buy a plot of land in the country and live the good life, while being prevented from achieving the dream of living a good life in order to create the wealth to achieve it. In the processes of attempting to achieve our own agendas we are confronted by competition and the threat from others pursuing their own agenda. The result is higher levels of anxiety and a perpetual restlessness, which destroys our ability to find peace, and the motion of this cycle intensifies as time goes on, making it harder to live by our values and beliefs. We stop being measured by the value of who we are and instead become judged by the market-dominated perspective of the value of what we do. "People must bear the full cost of choosing to work less, or in safer conditions, as a lower earning power relative to those who are willing to work flat-out (a matter of prudence). But also and primarily because only a certain kind of success is appreciated by the market and people do want to be successful" (Wells and Graafland, 2012). The result is that we have to choose between working longer hours to maintain our sense of self-value, while at the same time distorting our ability to understand the value of who we are beyond what we produce by making the choice to work longer hours.

The reality for most families in the UK today is a requirement for both parents to work. We can't afford to have Mum or Dad stay at home to look after the kids. We worry about how to heat our homes at winter because fuel prices are increasing year on year and the weekly food shop is getting difficult to afford. We can no longer afford to retire and even when we do, for most it will be retiring into poverty. At the same time, wages have stagnated and governments are engaging in an austerity program cutting public spending. Is it any wonder that 10 times more people suffer from depression now than in 1945? Adam Smith believed that the pursuit of a commercial society would deliver prosperity to the poor and bring economic and personal development benefits, natural justice, and freedom that would make capitalism worth defending. As we look at the world today, we must ask ourselves whether what we see is the freedom we were looking for as organizations continue in their pursuit of the profit agenda. The result appears to be broken homes and a broken society.

The economic crisis, decreasing wages in real terms, and inflationary pressure on basic products and services mean that the consumer has woken up to the fact that the dominance of money makes having more money essential for survival. Without it, life becomes impossible. As capitalism has globalized and monetization has permeated all areas of life, the predominance of illiberal values has increased and inequality has intensified. Neoliberalism has not increased growth rates; instead compared to the decades prior to 1980, growth has slowed for the economy as a whole, while the rich have seen their wealth increased rapidly during the same period (Monboit, 2016).

Globalization and Exploitation

Globalization may have increased the largesse of wealth, but its distribution has shrunk to a smaller percentage of the world's population. Although many attempts have been made to address the issues of inequality, most notably by numerous UN resolutions, the consequences of fast capitalism and the complexity and scale of global business mean the impact of good intentions based on voluntarism is limited. We are quickly approaching a tipping point where the problems of the capitalist illiberal principles at play in the system are resulting in catastrophic consequences. These consequences span the economy, political sphere, society, and the environment, and the impact they are having may threaten the future of human existence.

Globalization should, according to a liberal democratic tradition, represent a move toward a universality of wealth creation regardless of where an individual is from. However, the universality of wealth does not imply equality, but rather a level of proportionality. The problem with liberal capitalism is that it introduces a hierarchy that produces a gap so vast between rich and poor that inequality becomes accepted as a natural part of the democratic system. Furthermore, the rich West does not use its skills, knowledge, and resources to help enable the poor nations to transition quickly by using their wealth to develop essential infrastructure, such as advanced sanitation, health, and communication and transport networks, which would benefit the wider society. Instead governments represent business interests abroad and organizations seek to exploit the natural wealth resources of countries by focusing on the transactional nature of the capitalist system and investing the bare minimum required for operational reasons. Exploitation and deniability regarding criminality in the supply chain are part and parcel of modern business practice. The old saying about give a man a fish and he will feed his family for a day, teach a man to fish and he will feed his family forever, is never more appropriate. Charity may be given and wells may be dug, but what poor countries really need are assistance, technology, and knowledge that will enable them to build sewerage, water systems, safe housing, schools and health facilities, as well as agricultural support. The organizations that provide this are the not-for-profit and charitable organizations who see a need and try to help, but not in return for the countries' natural wealth. The organizations that exploit the wealth of third world countries are reluctant to invest for the long term in the communities in which they operate. Liberal capitalist globalization has led, therefore, to a system where production of goods and services in third world countries are directed by "disinterested markets and value-free capital in the direction of value-free outcomes" (Watson, 2004). The capitalist Western markets are not interested in globalization with the goal of creating equality of material wealth and prosperity to those places in the world that do not currently enjoy them. Instead corporations are seeking to reduce their cost base by transferring and outsourcing their operations to areas that have lower wages and lighter workforce regulations. Furthermore, they bring wealth only in regard to increasing the consumer market to which they can sell more services and products as growth begins to slow in their home markets. Globalization is not about spreading liberty and democracy but rather a continued expansion of corporate capitalism's control of the world's resources.

Globalization and "free" trade have created an imbalance both socially and environmentally. It is not just wealth that has been distributed unfairly, but the fact that the negative cost of our activities weighs most heavily on those least able to protect themselves from the excesses of others.

The Wealthocracy Replaces the Aristocracy

The trend toward monetization is demonstrated by the way employees and workers are being treated within the corporate workplace. The placement of employees on the corporate profit and loss has reduced their relationship to their corporate masters as little more than numbers on an accountant's spreadsheet that can be increased or reduced with minimal disruption to the decision-making process within the organization. As employees of a corporate machine, we have become depersonalized and dehumanized by the focus on money and numbers. Because of capitalism connection to liberal democracy and freedom, the oppression of the working classes is tolerated, because we are deemed to have the "choice" as to whom and where we sell our labor. With the abandonment of policies regarding the aim of full unemployment, the labor market has become a buyer's market. Workers who can find employment have to work harder, and there are fewer jobs available for them to exercise their choice of whom to sell their labor to. Increasing brutalization of the workplace is an indication that the balance of power has shifted to such a degree that employers no longer see their labor as value adding, but as a cost that needs to be controlled. Despite the human resource profession attempting to promote the need for employee engagement, the capitalist market has created a vicious circle where the majority of the population are paid low wages and therefore the products and services that they buy must service a low-cost structured economy. This in turn depreciates the amount, which organizations can afford to remunerate their employees, once again feeding the demand for low-cost goods and services.

Financialization has removed human society from that which is tangible to that which is little more than the religion of money, and in doing so has reduced human society to something that no longer holds any value beyond what wealth can be squeezed out of it. The naturalization of individualism has created a political and social dogma of self-interested behavior, which results in the competitive and egotistic pursuit of personal interest before social needs. We all compete to find our place, but in doing so we lose the ability to form alliances and demonstrate a social and class power that can demand and create change. Democracy today is little more than the juxtaposition of the wealthy asserting power over the running of government and society as a whole. A few years ago, then prime minister of the UK David Cameron claimed that we are all "classless" now. But the truth is there is the wealthy class and then there are the rest of us. The populist movement of 2016 sought to destroy this paradigm, leading to the political shocks of Brexit and a Trump presidency. However, Brexit is an act of national self-harm and Trump's cabinet has a net worth in excess of $14 billion. In a world that is more interconnected and interdependent than at any other time in history, we have created an environment in which capitalism seems to be a necessity for the continual functioning of society. But we must not mistake globalization as progress. Our society is controlled by

> less than three per cent of the world's population, namely the global capitalist core, [that] dominates the economic, monetary, financial and technological resources of the world in the name of free and open markets, democracy, rules-based fair trade and freedom. Roughly another twenty per cent produces most of the goods and services that gird this class-based democratic system, while very large portions of global humanity are forced to subsist at the margin, consistent with capitalism's historical tendencies of the concentration of income, assets and wealth in the hands of the relative few. (Watson, 2004)

By removing our identification with class power, capitalism not only robs us of the wealth we could and arguably, should have, but also creates an environment where we have been disempowered of our ability to struggle for equality.

The financialization of the market economy has meant that there has been an increasing level of inequality in regard to income since the early 1980s. Rather than reducing the gap between rich and poor, inequality has risen in the United States, the UK, and other rich countries. Those who contribute economic value in regard to tangible products, services, and knowledge have seen their financial value diminish at a time when intangible wealth in regard to stock prices, asset valuations, and capital gains has resulted in mega-wages and salaries paid to the city-rich. Furthermore, society has become infected with the diseases of the wealthy. If the financial markets are doing well, society experiences a boom; if the financial markets are doing badly, society suffers a crash. Society's well-being has become dependent on the unstable foundations of financial growth, which is based on the vagaries of market confidence, and our wellbeing is no longer determined by our productive capacity or intrinsic value but rather by the machinations of our financial overlords. Equity has replaced land as the new determination of power and riches.

Since the 1980s it has not been politics that has affected the lives of ordinary people; instead the fortunes of the wider population have become inextricably linked to the cycles and bubbles of the business cycle. These crises do not just affect the economic system, but have a major impact on our society. For each crisis that we suffer, we are confronted with significant societal upheavals, the destruction of manufacturing, the breakdown of local communities, political disruption, and slowdown in areas of societal development. Analysts will promote the ideas that the riches of the wealthiest will trickle down to those at the bottom of society, but the truth is that it is only a few who have the wealth and the trickle is barely a drip. Increasing levels of instability, inequality in the areas of income, wealth, and power means that the cost is borne by those at the bottom of the society, and the prizes are being enjoyed by those at the very top. But this cycle cannot continue endlessly. As wealth is driven further and further away from those who can generate value in the economy, the illusion of prosperity begins to grow transparent. The subprime mortgage market, the deck of cards that the equity markets are playing, is no longer generating growth as the wider population deals not only with recession but rising prices.

The financial system needs consumers to consume more in order to drive growth, but the extent of the inequality in incomes and the cost of the 2008 financial collapse to the wider society has meant that there is no stretch left in the consumers' "knicker elastic"—it is no longer plausible to expect the worst off to drive economic growth.

An output of the capitalist agenda is that everything has a price, "everything has been monetised and any other currency is systematically belittled. If labour is not specifically valuable in a financial marketplace— i.e. profitable—then it is labour without 'real' value . . . one sees the ghastly consequences of this inversion of human value everywhere" (Orr, 2012). The joke that a financier would "even sell his grandmother if there was a profit to be made" is becoming too close to the truth.

The Economics of Politics

The issues of our current system are more than simply the way we do business, but they are in the very structure of our democracy itself. In the UK we have adapted our system over a period of centuries and are left with a system, which is an anachronism. History has left an indelible mark on the way in which our political and economic institutions operate. Self-interested capitalism taps into the remnants of colonialism and the social impact is that of a disconnect between the human condition and a passivity of those who could mediate change, remaining alienated from the problems and issues that affect people outside of their domain. The pursuit of private ends for private means subjects us all to a blind acceptance that it is not our problem. Capitalism and liberalism did not save Western society from its feudal or colonial past, but instead it has extended the operation of such structures from land-based wealth to capital-based wealth before finally succumbing to where we are today, power held by the wealthy elite. They are the modern-day equivalent of the feudal knights or colonial overlords, who now rule and suppress using financial wealth, which is not necessarily linked to any tangible products or anything that is "real." Even those who have the biggest property portfolio have lost their position of dominance to those with the best performing investment portfolio, many of which do not relate to anything other than a mix of financial products that exist purely on paper. But society cannot be built on paper and social ills cannot be improved by placing value on the shuffling of "shares" that in reality have no more substance than a deck of cards. The reason why so many people can lose their fortunes on the merry-go-round called the stock market is that there is no basis to their wealth other than confidence and belief.

Government and big business would have us believe that we have never had it so good, that even though we are experiencing economic austerity and wage stagnation, it is just a blip in our continuing improvement in lifestyle. But just as we have begun to understand the enormity of the devastation we have wreaked on planet earth in our pursuit of profit, so too we have begun to understand that society has also been robbed of true prosperity.

Even in the so-called communist states, the pursuit of power and then the holding onto power ultimately became about the economic advantages having power gives to the power holder. Mao, Saddam, Castro, Mugabe, Putin, Mubarak, and Gaddafi,—their grip on power was not and has never been about politics but the economic advantages bestowed on the position they hold. Furthermore, the misuse of political power is as damaging to equality and society as the current misuse of economic power. It may begin as a social endeavor, but it often ends with coercion and abuse of power, which is destructive and fails to deliver an agenda other than the inevitable self-interest required of capitalism.

Political systems are struggling as governments become focused on retaining power. In the UK, the government is governing with a mandate of less than 50 percent of electorate support, and the current Prime Minister Theresa May has never been to the polls as the leader of the Conservative Party. The electorate quite rightly believes that politicians serve themselves, rather than the people they were elected to serve. The sovereign debt crisis is a result of governments mortgaging the long-term stability of the country they govern in return for short-term popularity.

The Socio-Environmental Cost

But society is not the only casualty of profit. The natural environment has been occupied, harvested, and plundered, since the beginning of industrialization, including the clearing of communities that had been living in harmony with the land, all in the name of progression.

> We have destroyed forests, topsoil and farmland and with those the habitat for many species. The loss of biological diversity has been matched by the loss of cultural diversity . . . The waste of

natural capital is matched by waste of human capital: vast numbers of unemployed and over a billion of us today, severely malnourished, many starving. (Mayer, 2007)

The exploitative relationship is not restricted to organizational life, but rather is reproduced throughout society and the wider environment (Torrington, 1993). The pursuit of "ambition and self-seeking effort" promoted by the ideas of Adam Smith has meant that capitalism has achieved increased wealth and prosperity, but not for all; rather, for the minority (Cunningham, 2004). Self-interest has resulted in poor stewardship of the earth's natural resources threatening water supplies, reducing food production, and increasing the instability of the natural environment impacting our towns and cities. Child poverty, pedophilia, homelessness, prostitution, human trafficking, and modern slavery all exist and are on the increase in capitalist economies, the land of the wealthy West and the land of the free.

An Amoral System

But it is more than simple economics that makes capitalism so difficult to tackle. The capitalist economic system is ideologically linked to democracy. Workers are free to sell their labor to the highest bidder, and in return receive an income and benefits for their efforts. The argument goes that the market has natural checks and balances that mean that society and its members are better off. Adam Smith himself explored the need for these checks and balances in his book *The Theory of Moral Sentiments*, where self-interest is balanced by man's ability to form moral judgments.

But capitalism is morally agnostic. For 30 years, the growing persuasiveness of the pursuit of individual self-interest and the idea that people should have the freedom to make their own choices have eroded our ability to impose moral judgments on others and have been messing with our ethical and moral compass. The application of being nonjudgmental in the face of personal self-interest has contributed to a societal moral malaise. What is considered right and what is wrong have given way to a passive acceptance that all things are permissible, as long as they are aligned with capitalist values. Take the case of an individual who was jailed for seven months following the summer riots in the UK in 2011. His crime was to encourage others to riot on Facebook, a riot that never did take place and yet not a single person has been jailed for the part they played in creating the 2008 banking crisis.

By maintaining an amoral approach to competition, players can choose to follow only the rules that help them win. If honesty and fairness raise costs, without producing a valuable return, then there is no rationale for remaining honest or fair. Different benchmarks arise in regard to what standards are acceptable. If actions, regardless of their morality, produce profit with no consequence, it is logical that other players in the marketplace will adopt those practices in order to remain competitive. The 2017 United Airlines social media exposure regarding the removal of a fare-paying passenger has highlighted a previously accepted industry practice of removing consumers who have paid for a seat involuntarily from flights. It is only the bad PR and reputational damage that is causing the airline introspection regarding the practice. Therefore, capitalism completely ignores any moral obligations we have to those who will be affected by our decisions and actions. But in any civil society, it is necessary to consider the interests of all stakeholders, and that means there is a requirement for moral decision-making. No decision that affects others can be protected by a belief in self-interest alone. Although we possess the power to make our own decisions, propriety dictates that the power to choose must be balanced with responsibility toward the interests of others in the wider context.

In a system where self-interest rules, social norms of right and wrong lose objective validity; they become important only relative to the individual. Consequently, capitalism's protection of self-interest elevates each of us to be the sole and final judge of what is right and wrong, guarding the individual's right to make a self-interested decision, regardless of whether it is dishonest, irresponsible, or damaging to society at large.

Following the banking crisis of 2008, it has become apparent that the reality of capitalism is different from the benign myth of the protector of freedom and democracy, and moral judgment has become lost in the pursuit of self-interest. Rather than a democratic outcome where all benefit, the rich and powerful are being served by the majority and the common man is slave to the mighty corporation. Unable to break free from low wages, restricted in their ability to achieve their potential and suffering from poor education, the exploitation of the poor continues, but under the guise of contracted hours and a job description.

Criminal activities are increasingly linked to the purposeful malfeasance toward the vulnerable in society. Despite slavery being officially abolished worldwide in 1981, modern slavery and trafficking continues unabated. The Trafficking in Persons Report 2015 identified 44,462 victims of forced prostitution, slavery, and labor trafficking in 2015 and the International Labour Organization (2016) estimates that forced labor generates profits of $150 billion per annum with 21 million victims of forced labor at any one time. This is double the number of the 10.24 million enslaved Africans who arrived in the Americas between 1650 and 1900 and just one example of the lack of moral judgment in the market-led economy.

The criminal exploitation of people in the pursuit of profit is not a new phenomenon, and in an ideological debate many may argue that it is overly emotional to compare the machinations of today's organizations with the slave trade. But, aside from illegal slavery, organizations and specifically the financial institutions that are the beating heart of the capitalist system are little different from the colonial slave traders of the eighteenth century. Brunsson (2015) states that "the United Nations (UN) declaration of human rights, which states that all human beings are born free and equal in dignity and rights (1948: Article 1), is ignored because, within organisations, it becomes obvious that people are indeed unequal." It may not be systemized, it may not be open, but the exploitation of human beings is alive and well, except it is now called strategic human resource management.

Ask a manager what the extra bank holiday is going to cost the business and he'll reel off a number, ask him what value spending time with family and friends has to his workers, and you'll get a response accusing you of having a screw loose. It's easy to find the cost of training in an organization since it would be a simple case of looking in the right ledger. But if you were to try to find out the value of human potential and talent in an organization, the answer would be impossible to find—we don't measure value, we only measure cost.

Zero hours contracts, bullying in the workplace, outsourcing to countries that don't practice the same workforce protections, child labor, long hours culture, burgeoning wage gap, unequal pay, and health and safety violations, they go on all the time. These ethical violations are justified because of the economic climate and because the organization needs to be efficient. But in the pursuit of "growth," we are living in times of moral hazard.

The Pursuit of Growth

Capitalists would argue that growth is necessary for the greater good, but the economist Richard Easterlin in his paper "Does Economic Growth Improve the Human Lot?" "Concluded after a thorough survey of happiness and GNP in a number of countries" that the answer was "probably, no" (Skidelsky and Skidelsky, 2012). The paper was published in 1974 and it is interesting to note that life satisfaction has not increased at all since that time. Despite our lives changing immeasurably in terms of material acquisition, wealth does not impact positively on how happy we are. Furthermore, growth doesn't guarantee that everyone will find or enjoy employment. "Unemployment in Europe was very low from the end of the Second World War to the end of the 1960s. Since then it has increased through shocks and recessions, while falling little in years of growth" (Galbraith, 2012). For young people entering today's workplace, prospects are worse than they have ever been. Graduates, despite their qualifications, are forced to decide whether to accept a low-wage job, which has little relation to their studies, and in doing so, possibly restricting themselves to continuing low-paid employment. Or they may choose to wait for a "better" job that may or may not materialize in the hope that they can begin their career in a higher paying role. There are a growing percentage of 16–25-year-olds that are neither in education, training, or employment, increasing the likelihood of them never being a productive member of society.

Our governments now look to growth as being the answer to our present austerity woes, despite all the evidence showing that it was the pursuit of growth and the love of finance, of and for itself, that led the majority suffering at the folly of the few; "new data suggest[s], instead, that macroeconomics—global macroeconomics, with an emphasis on financial governance and financial instability—is the correct framework for coherently explaining the relationship between inequality, unemployment and growth" (Galbraith, 2012). Those in power continue to plunder and get rich, while justifying their existence by insisting that the markets can deliver the freedom from oppression. The sad truth is that Thatcherism and Reaganomics introduced the cultural acceptance of income inequality and the promotion of a market-led system that meant that "individuals were no longer to be viewed as part of wholes; the wholes were simply the sum of individual parts" (Skidelsky and Skidelsky, 2010). Governments no longer run the economy, nor do the central banks; instead it is organizations and "the market" that produce the framework upon which our economic fortunes are made or lost. Moral and social restraint has been removed from the equation. If a course of action doesn't make sense for the bottom line, it doesn't make sense.

The Rise of the Corporate State

The dominance of Greek rationalist thinking and the drive for efficiency have commoditized and dehumanized our society. Management theory taught in business schools across the world teaches managers that the pursuit of shareholder value and efficiency is the primary purpose of organizations. Most management theory has been developed only in the last 100 years, and whether it is bureaucratic or post-bureaucratic, scientific or humanist in flavor, the driving theme is that the purpose of management is the pursuit of better economic performance for the organization and return on investment for its shareholders.

The neoliberal democratic politics of Western cultures and the capitalist economic model and the resulting ideological link with societal notions of democratic freedom prevent governments and organizations from pursuing an ethical and values-driven agenda that furthers the health and wellbeing of society if it conflicts with the short-term delivery of return on investment. Neoliberal policy advocates that government avoids the pursuit of socially conscious policies, instead creating a soft regulatory framework and deregulation that "is good for business" in order to compete globally with other sovereign states.

The muscular entrepreneurialism promoted by Thatcher and Reagan and the drive toward principles of voluntarism have had a major impact on both politics and sociocultural values. "Neoliberalism sees competition as the defining characteristic of human relations. It redefines citizens as consumers, whose democratic choices are best exercised by buying and selling, a process that rewards merit and punishes inefficiency" (Monbiot, 2016). Deregulation was a cornerstone of both the Reagan administration and the Thatcher government, set on the belief that government interference was making the economy weak and disrupting the free market mechanisms. The political elite of the European Union enthusiastically copied the American model of a liberalized labor market, "jettisoning job protections, cutting unemployment insurance, and weakening unions . . . and free wages to adjust to new patterns of supply and demand" (Galbraith, 2012).

In the decades since, self-interest and individual rights have replaced responsibility, and a business-first interest has been prioritized as a consequence of the adoption of a market-outsider model of corporate governance in the UK. The result has been that top managers are rewarded and penalized only on market-based measures of success and isolating the transactional nature of interaction between organization and shareholder from the wider societal context in which the organization operates. There is no noble cause or pursuit of a higher purpose; instead there is only the market and continuing machinations of want and endless pursuit of more wealth, with no consideration as to what more wealth will achieve. Money in and of itself has no intrinsic value, other than what the person who is receiving money deems it to be worth, and so inflation and currency fluctuations can devalue the money that we have labored for.

In recent years, rather than protection provided by the state, it has instead been the rise of "corporate socialism" that has delivered notions such as holistic, organic, sustainable, motivational, diverse, equal opportunity, developmental, and corporate social responsibilities. A recognition, it seems, by organizations that a purely economic agenda has flaws and that people don't like to be exploited and will resist control. It is extraordinary that economics has become "the theology of our age, the language that all interests, high and low, must speak if they are to win a respectful hearing in the courts of power. Economics owes it special position in part of the failure of other disciplines to impress their stamp on political debate" (Skidelsky and Skidelsky, 2012). For those in positions of power and on the receiving end of wealth, there is a tendency to worship at the altar of the market. The super-rich believe themselves to be God-like in their ability to make money and yet they do not create, they do not preserve life; instead they build empires that have their foundations on numbers, trends, and statistics.

What is most worrying is that it is business that is driving the social agendas of our age. Environmental concerns have only recently been given credence and a voice, not because their quality of argument has improved since the 1960s, but rather because organizations have a self-interest in protecting value resources so that they continue to pursue wealth creation. Programs to support youth and community projects are geared to securing future employees, ensuring that the organization has a reliable source of skills and knowledge to employ, as well as securing favorable PR and developing a loyal customer base. Employee reward programs and diversity programs are approved if there is a business case demonstrating "going the extra mile" discretionary behavior, employee engagement, greater productivity, and a return on investment.

However, despite many trying to fight the good fight and organizations and governments talking about ethical business, the truth is that many organizations outsource parts of the operation for economic reasons to other companies that run sweatshops or practice abhorrent work practices. Management teams learn about the importance of motivation to get the best out of people, but will still increase their own wages by 50 percent, while freezing the pay of their employees. Their reasoning based on having been taught that as long as people have enough to live on, money doesn't motivate them to go the extra mile and a corporate social responsibility agenda will only be followed as long as it makes economic sense for the organization to do so.

The Devaluation of Human Life

In Greece, hundreds of families were forced to abandon their children because they can no longer look after them, while the European Union insists on austerity measures in response to Greece's debt crisis. Yet the Greek prime minister was forced to resign and a referendum result ignored so that the EC, IMF, and ECB could force bail out conditions upon the country. In Syria children are tortured by government forces and over 470,000 people have been killed in response to the rebellion against the Assad regime while the United Nations argues over whether to get involved or not. There were 5,098 migrant deaths recorded in the Mediterranean Sea in 2016, a total of over 12,000 deaths since 2014, and the European Union's response has been to create a new Border and Coast Guard Agency. The millions of people fleeing Afghanistan, Iraq, and Syria by sea are classed as migrants, yet they are fleeing war, poverty, and oppression. The European Union is avoiding the legal ramifications of acknowledging the refugee crisis in order to justify closed borders and the inhumane and miserable conditions these victims of one of the biggest humanitarian crisis since the Second World War are being subjected to.

Not a single person will look at these figures and not think that this is tragic, that the values of human society have somehow got mixed up and yet every day we continue to take part in a system, making decisions that "devalue" people to be defined by a statistic. Rather than improving long-term prosperity, in the longest period of peace in the continent's history, the European Union is struggling with sovereign debt, a financial crisis, and a movement of people that is threatening its very survival.

But instead of the refugee crisis calling to the humanity of those who should be reaching out to help, the reaction has been isolation, nationalism, fear, and loathing. Migrants are spat at, abused, and degraded, while the politicians adopt an agenda that places the blame for the failings of the capitalist system onto the shoulders of people who need our help. Our infrastructure is failing, social services are being reduced, and our wages depressed because of "them" instead of because of organizations paying profits to shareholders, fat cat pay, and lack of capital investment in projects, which have a long-term return on investment and benefit the wider society instead of the wealthy elite.

Other inequalities exist. The UK legal system protects property over people. Fraud is a more serious crime than rape, abuse, or murder, and even animals have more rights and protection than children. Our education system continues to fail our children and prevents them from being able to recognize their talent and abilities at an early age. Instead it promotes passive learning in order to pass tests rather than learning to think independently and encourages individuals to opt out because they don't "fit" what is considered to be important at school but of little use in working life. Most damning is that our society fails to protect the vulnerable. Pension provision is in crisis, prisons are bursting at the seams, homelessness is increasing, mental health patients are abandoned to the community, and the health service runs a postcode lottery.

Parents buy their children's affection through showering them with material goods, family holidays and leisure time are interrupted because of work commitments, communities have been destroyed because of plant, and office closures and urban areas and cities have become ghost towns in the name of profit and progress

For every CEO and politician that "gets it," there are many that nod their heads at the need for better government and better business, but fail to learn the lessons from the 2008 credit crunch. They plough on the fact that "more spending" is needed as if continual consumption is the only solution to the world problems. The fact that the pursuit of monetarism policies is the reason why the capitalist system finally imploded seems to have escaped our leaders.

Which Leads Us to Conclude . . .

But what if capitalism and the market economy, in its current form, is the wrong model for the pursuit of fulfilling the needs of human society and organizational performance? What if the current capitalist system and a laissez-faire philosophy, is inadequate to solve the problems in the world economy resulting from the credit crunch, mass migration, global recession, and the emergence of unsustainable sovereign debt?

Society is crumbling, the growing level of civil unrest and rise of populism are a warning of what will happen if change does not occur and yet despite the credit crunch, Brexit, and Trump our political and organizational leaders are still not changing course. More and more evidence is appearing that demonstrates that the course that we have pursued for the last three decades is responsible for the ills in society. Many individuals have raised their concerns and have been treated as if they were being irrational, as if the pursuit of consumerism and material wealth in some way excuses the acceptance of inequality as a necessary evil. Capitalists will argue that the lives of workers in the Western world have improved compared to a hundred years ago, that our standard of living is as a direct result of pursuing market-led policies. But our rise in living standards has not been a result of the pursuit of a market-led agenda by organizations. It wasn't the market that delivered a universal health service, pursued equality, sought out better working conditions, and secured the minimum wage. These things would not have been achieved if the market had been left unregulated. Even with intervention the statistics are challenging to the "capitalism is good" brigade. Thirty-three percent of the UK population are qualified as living in poverty; the UK is number two in the OECD for wage inequalities, the United States number one; wage growth continues to stagnate and the UKCES 2015 reported that 23 percent of vacancies are hard to fill due to lack of skills. And yet, according to the Institute of Policy Studies, in 2009 "the average CEO of a big company made 411 times the wages of an average worker . . . that's roughly 10 times the proportion in 1980" (CQ Researcher, 2010). Lancaster University Management School shows that "the median pay for chief executives at Britain's 350 biggest companies was £1.9m in 2014—a rise of 82% in 11 years . . . However, performance as measured by return on capital invested was less than 1% during that period" (BBC, 2016). With over two billion individuals living on less than $2 per day, the greatest social challenge we face is that of addressing poverty, and it cannot be addressed if government, organizations, and individuals continue to withhold "a reasonable share of their resources, skills and know-how to jointly achieve sustainable solutions" (Leisinger, 2007). In capitalism there will always be losers; the issue that faces us today is that the number of winners is reducing and the losers represent society as a whole.

But organizations are not bad in and of themselves. They are inevitable in human society; they are not merely a social construction but a scientific reality of the human spirit and a universal truth of the human condition. Place groups of humans together and they will form cooperatives and organize themselves, whether in primitive or advanced forms. Brunsson (2015) highlights that "organisations are so dominant that Herbert Simon (1991) suggested the term 'organizational economy' should be substituted for the often used 'market economy.'" Regardless of politics or a public or private agenda, organizations exist and society forms, and therefore organizations have a specific and important role to play in human society, politics, and our economic wellbeing.

But is the pursuit of an economic agenda inevitable too? Return on investment, supply and demand, operational efficiency, profit and loss, shareholder value—are these deliverables the only purposes that organizations can pursue? Are market forces and capitalism inevitable? Or do democracies pursue the wrong agenda because they believe it is the only agenda?

CHAPTER 4

Introducing a Different Agenda—Temperatism

The best state for human nature is that in which, while no one is poor, no one desires to be richer, nor has any reason to fear from being thrust back, by the efforts of others to push themselves forward.

—John Mill

The original temperance social movement emerged in the late eighteenth century in the United States, spreading to other Western societies with members seeking a reduction or prohibition of the consumption of alcoholic beverages, with drunkenness a direct result of the social problems in society. Temperance is often described as a virtue, whereby the individual avoids being overcome by temptation and moderates wants within the boundary of propriety, modesty, and good health. In this sense, Adam Smith himself considered temperance as a "natural liberty" that enables society to prosper. Individuals are responsible for controlling their own consumption, but equally are supported by a culture that esteems those who behave with temperance. Individuals therefore develop a high personal reputation by developing prudence and moral decency in regard to their behavior and thus become valued by society for qualities that are worthy of recognition. "Smith considered that the 'social market' for temperance would tend to encourage frugality, since spectators are more likely to disapprove of any small impropriety (in spending more than one has, or eating voraciously in public) than excessive propriety" (Wells and Graafland, 2012). The Victorian Temperance movement was a response to the increase in alcohol-related issues, with violence toward women and children. The resulting degradation caused by the working man falling into alcoholism became more evident as the Industrial Revolution began to transform the Victorian society. Today society once again is experiencing the problems of rapid industrialization in emerging economies and the dramatic impact resulting from the digital revolution and globalization over the past 25 years. Government policies and societal structures reflect the economic demands of capitalism, protecting those with wealth and property and supporting a self-interested and individualist approach to governance.

The promotion of deregulation during the 1980s led directly to the excesses in the world economy that produced the 2008 credit crunch. Furthermore, the growth of consumerism and self-interest as societal norms is delivering a deathblow to the glue that binds human society together. Temperance as a virtue clashes with the commercial society in which we live, frugality isn't rewarded, and excess is celebrated. Individuals now have to find their own balance of restraint. Rather than support temperance in the face of recession, the social and economic system continues to push consumers to spend. In the midst of recession, politicians and business leaders debate over which method is most likely to get the consumer spending again. Temperance has diminished in direct relation to the growth of consumption and the need for consumers to have material possessions to secure their place and perceived value in society, while becoming the engine of the economy. Abundance and free choice present the modern-day consumer with a "child in a sweetie shop" mentality, where self-regulation becomes nigh on impossible because of the variety of temptations on offer. Organizations compete by providing consumers excuses to indulge. The marketing slogan is deliberately designed to entice us to believe that we are worth "it" whatever "it" is that the organization is selling.

Our lives have become a cycle of keeping up with the Jones and the need to be in possession of the latest gadgets and gizmos to remain relevant. Until the credit crunch, the provision of cheap credit provided consumers with the means with which to indulge in unabashed consumption. This behavior was a symptom of the big shift that capitalism has taken in the last few decades, moving from the sphere of an economic mechanism into a market system designed to produce, deliver, and service every pleasure imaginable for our consumption. Necessity no longer drives forward our economy, nor is it the basis for motivation in individuals. Instead we pursue desire, conformity, and the cult of self-expression as our new measure of economic achievement. For many, our drive to consume is the paragon of the capitalist creed of self-interest. But rather than demonstrate our individualism, we use our material possessions to enhance our social standing and increase our acceptability within our social groups. We are all converts to the religion of consumerism, but the indoctrination of materialism is dehumanizing us all in a corrupt cycle of transaction and commerce. "Rampant consumerism, globalization and the decline of many institutions and fixed points in society have given rise to . . . isolated individuals occupying increasingly atomised existences" (Clegg, 2016: 250). Even organizations are being tempted to indulge, as the market promotes the need for organizations to become involved in their own personal shopping sprees: acquisitions, mergers, and takeovers. In the last decade temperance was especially lacking in the finance sector, where propriety and prudence were replaced with greed and excessive risk taking, driven by a desire to be recognized for delivering bigger results and more spectacular deals than competitors.

Just as the original temperance movement highlighted that alcohol can be injurious to physical and psychological health, so too are the excesses of the capitalist system. "Money is just a cargo cult, one that has been wrongly and willfully elevated to the status of a pseudo-science. 'Confidence' is what economists call willingness to spend, even as they destroy the confidence of so many people by leaving the market to inform them that they are not worth much and never will be" (Orr, 2012). The societal problems caused by the worldwide recession have affected those lower down the social spectrum more than those near the top. The poor are quite literally getting poorer, while the rich get richer. Something needs to change if people are to be protected, not just in regard to their security, but to improve their working and living conditions and avoid the continuation of the domination and exploitation that they have been exposed to via the growth of capitalism and the capitalist class.

Darkness Before the Dawn

Politicians and business leaders would have us believe that the only way out of the economic turmoil is through more deregulation, smaller government, less welfare, and tax reform so businesses can be more competitive and the rich and powerful can create and secure jobs. "As Margaret Thatcher once put it, not only is capitalism good, 'There is no alternative.'" Monbiot (2016) suggests that "so pervasive has neoliberalism become that we seldom even recognize it as an ideology . . . we internalize and reproduce its creeds." This effort to present managerial capitalism as universal and as necessary has been roundly criticized by a range of critics . . . it has become all but unthinkable to imagine anything more than minor changes in the social structure or economic systems" (Stokes, 2011). The ability of capitalism to mark any opposition as anti-democratic, or an infringement of liberal traditions, makes any attempt to search for an alternative fraught with difficulties. There are any number of individuals and groups writing reports and making arguments for change. But these ideas struggle to gather momentum. Even where direct action is taken, as in the Occupy movement, the wider public does not hear the arguments, the action is considered to be a nuisance, and, in the case of the Wall Street Occupy Movement, a public menace. With politics dominated by variations of capitalism in their economic discourse, universities filled with economists who teach capitalism to their students, and corporations unable to operate outside of the capitalist market system, the noise created demanding change becomes nothing more than a humming in the background. The problem with different being dismissed as impossible is that different is exactly what is needed right now if the human race is to avoid the fate of the dodo.

For many there is a curiosity of human irrationality that makes them wonder why we find ourselves in a position of empowered and disempowered, rich and poor, and the continuation of behavior that will lead to our eventual demise. But revisiting the history of Western democracy and liberalism demonstrates that there is any number of examples lying in the wastes of civility that demonstrate the ability of man to act against the interests of the wider society, exploit the weak, and coerce the poor for their own means. What we ignore at our peril is the fate of all great civilizations that, having stretched their resources to a breaking point, find themselves reduced in a couple of decades. The once vast Roman Empire disappeared in as little as 50 years as it exceeded its ability to live within its means and the boundaries of its resources. But our own self-destruction is not destined. Alongside each failure is an example of humanity's ability to change fundamentally the way in which we operate. Two hundred years ago abolitionists tackled the appalling colonial slave trade and the accompanying genocide of whole generations of Africans caught up in slavery. Human society has been dogged by racial oppression, class struggle, and gender inequality, but all the while making progress through civil rights movements, trade unionism, and feminism. We may look at history in despair at man's ability to act in an undemocratic manner, especially where there is money to be made, property rights to be protected, and wealth to be created. Or we can note that for each abhorrent waste of human talent and potential we have fought for freedom from coercion and greater liberty. What once began as a movement to exclude or remove sections of society, became a moment in history where a great leap forward was made in regard to liberty, freedom, and civilization for more people. We may yet be a long way off from true equality, and in regard to wealth distribution, the West is more unequal than even three decades ago. But it is always darkest before the dawn, and such is the level of inequality that once again humanity stirs from its slumber and begins to question the way things are and imagine the way that things could and should be.

An Alternative

Temperatism as an ideology offers more than a moderate form of capitalism. Many politicians today have expressed a need for "responsible" capitalism, and Jeff Randall when reporting the Libor scandal on Sky News suggested that it was time to stop worshipping at the mountain of Mammon (Material Wealth and Greed). Though the world has moved on from the world of Gordon Gekko, a seed was sown in the 1980s that has determined the course of human history to bring us to the financial crisis, global depression, and political instability that we find ourselves in today. The reality is that the range of options available to Western society in regard to a response to the problems that we are experiencing appears limited, and different combinations of regulations and deregulations have been tried to combat the impact of boom and bust of the capitalist market. Gordon Brown, then UK Chancellor of the Exchequer, proclaimed the "end of boom and bust" while presiding over the biggest consumer debt and spending bubble and the largest financial market bust in capitalism's history. There is an assumption that in a marketplace of good economic ideas capitalism has emerged as the best ideology after a fair fight, even if it is a poor one in regard to solving long-term societal problems and the exploitation of the poor by the rich. But to believe there is no alternative is to forget about how enterprising, innovative, and inventive the human race can be when faced with a fight for its own survival.

What globalization has produced is the means by which change can take place and take place quickly. We already have at our disposal the technical means to create a global society, which is free of want. Developments in technology and science means that for the first time in history we can develop an infrastructure that would support food production, healthcare, and education to create a society free of want, on the basis of the need for a minimum standard required to live well. Of course the capitalist core, those in the top percentile, will argue and proactively work against such a possibility, because they do not wish to weaken their control over the system, nor reduce their own wealth in the pursuit of the eradication of the need of and benefit for others. How can we be sure this will happen? Could it be that the means already exist by which the wealthy can volunteer "doing good" activities, which can create an abundance required to meet basic needs? Why is it that some become involved in philanthropic acts, while many do not?

The main problem we face is that the purpose of capitalism is the pursuit of profit. So organizations and individuals pursuing profit regardless of social cost or putting profit before people *is* "responsible" capitalism. They are doing what capitalism seeks to achieve. Any organization that wants to compete in our current economic framework must compete with others not only to meet the existing needs of consumers, but also to create in the mind of the consumers wants that they have yet to think of, in order that the organization can succeed in creating greater levels of additional consumption. Thirty years ago smartphones; instant, stable, and fast access to the Internet; and digital downloads weren't "wanted" by consumers. But now these things are "normal" wants. Consumers want to be connected, they want to be able to carry, listen, and read their digital libraries wherever they go, and producers are in a battle to ensure we have the devices and means to be able to do that. As we grow up and become more mobile because of an increasingly competitive job market, our wants and needs change further. Convenience is necessary because we need things to be convenient to fit in with our busy lifestyle. It is not efficient in regard to natural resources and creates a headache in regard to biodegradable waste, but it has become necessary, as our social and geographic mobility has increased. To speak temperance in regard to personal consumption into such an environment is challenging. For any individual they can reason as to why their materialism is necessary, why their excess of material goods is essential and indeed appropriate given their budget, and the way in which they operate their lives. We can all justify what we have and what we aspire to have. We persuade ourselves that the items that clutter our homes are what we ought to have and essential to our survival. But in a society driven by consumption and a market mechanism which is constantly creating new wants and turning wants into normal needs, it is increasingly difficult to separate how much is enough and what our real needs are, which is why temperance is a necessity if change, real change, is to occur. Developing a modern non-subjective, socially enforced framework regarding consumption standards will be a necessary starting point, if capitalism is to be overturned.

A New Way to Think About Business

In choosing the term *Temperatism* for the introduction of a people-centric approach to thinking about business and doing good, it is important to explore the many definitions of the word *temperate*, which include:

- Moderate and self-restrained; not extreme in opinion or statement
- Moderate in regard to indulgence of appetite or passion
- Not excessive in degree, as things, qualities, etc.
- Moderate in respect to temperature; not subject to prolonged extremes of hot or cold weather.

Moderation is a term that many commentators are currently using in arguments regarding the sustainability of capitalism, but trying to persuade a capitalist system to operate with moderation is akin to asking, as the early temperance movement did, an alcoholic to promise not to drink spirits, while still being able to continue consuming wine and beer. The injurious nature of the relationship between the alcoholic and alcohol wasn't changed, just moved from one form of abuse to another. In an attempt to keep a grip on power, many may argue that it is possible to change capitalism through a number of structural reforms to corporate boards, or threatening those who do not act moderately with legal restraints or additional regulation regarding corporate governance. But more regulation, or greater policing of the way in which organizations operate, will only ever be a partial solution to the problems created by capitalism.

> No amount of government intervention can alone adequately substitute for what Adam Smith called "temperance, decency, modesty and moderation." The behaviour of corporate executives in a number of instances suggests that we are faced with a collapse of a sense of "enoughness," of constraints on behaviour that were once imposed by conventional morality. What has been lost is the fact that the very preservation of the system requires that executives behave with moderation. (Stelzer, 2004)

To ask a capitalist to moderate their pursuit of profit while still allowing them to pursue a profit agenda will not reduce the problems of capitalism during a period of unprecedented change in a rapidly industrializing and globalized world economy. The more self-interested we have become, the more the goal of getting rich for the sake of being rich possesses us. We have lost from our society a great deal of understanding regarding a sense of decency and honor in the way in which we treat and value our fellow man. Individualism works only one way and that is not in a way that aligns itself with values such as social thinking, environmentalism, equality, poverty eradication, and true democratic freedom.

Temperatism is a new way to think about business and doing good, which pulls on a number of ideas in regard to economic, social, and political goals, the type of expectations that we should have of one another and the suggestion of some actions that could be taken to tackle the problems caused by capitalism. To some the ideas might appear abstract, such as the notion of doing good. But when applied to social, economic, political, and environmental issues, the concepts come to life. As with every approach to business, Temperatism is very explicit as a system of thought stemming from the virtue of temperance. There is a foundation of thinking based on the expectation of propriety in the social standards that should be set in our activities. Temperatism is focused on the outcomes of our political, economic, and social behaviors. It promotes an entitlement to basic human rights, a minimum standard of living that is acceptable and opportunities for all individuals to exercise their talent capability to reach their potential. Individuals, organizations, and government will be held to account for the decisions they make and the outcome of such decisions in the framework of the betterment of human society as a whole. Those who contribute by doing good will be rewarded for their efforts, while everyone in society will be empowered to take part in a democratic and equitable process that reduces differences in the proportion of reward one receives for effort and value-adding contributions.

Unlike other business approaches Temperatism isn't seeking to control the means of production, or indeed manipulate market prices, or prevent free competition. Instead Temperatism is seeking that the primary goal and agenda of the economic marketplace and organizations be changed to that of doing good, to adopt an ethical and values-based system of economic, social, and political participation. To put social needs above self-interest, Temperatism offers an alternative that goes against capitalist ideology and liberal tradition in the Western world. For individuals, the pursuit of temperance and the creation of a discipline in avoiding excessive indulgence in consumption seek to create an environment where kindness, support, and togetherness reconnect them with other people and the community in which they reside. For organizations, although no business would openly state that they seek to destroy lives, manipulate, and exploit, it is their actions rather than their words, the outcomes of their behavior, that demonstrate where their values really lie.

Therefore, the reason why the word *Temperatism* has been chosen for this proposed new approach to business is in regard to the position of *teetotalism toward a consumption and profit pursuant agenda*. Only abstinence from the pursuit of the capitalist agenda can be said to work in eliminating the negative outcomes we are currently experiencing. Attempts by sovereign nations to tailor capitalist economic treatments to different cultures have all led to the same outcome, harm, and waste. At its heart, Temperatism seeks to change the dominant agenda from the capitalist model of the "pursuit of profit" to that of "doing good." Many may frown at the use of such a subjective word. What after all constitutes "good" and how can it be understood and positioned in such a way that is universally, culturally, and socially acceptable and more importantly something that decisions can be made on, plans formed, and actions taken.

CHAPTER 5

Doing Good and What That Means

Faith in responsibility, belief in opportunity, and ability to unite around common values are what makes this nation great.
—Barack Obama

At this point it is pertinent to remind the readers that the purpose of this book is not to provide them with all the answers, but to create a debate about a possible alternative. Consider for yourself what a doing good agenda might involve and question what alternatives might be appropriate in the context of an antithesis to the profit agenda currently pursued by capitalism. Defining "doing good" for society at this stage of debate would be rather like the author suggesting what good food is. It is a matter of taste and up for discussion. However, as an offering as a foundation of a new way to think about business, there are universal truths as to what "good" constitutes regardless of the cultural, social, or economic background that you occupy. It is therefore important in proposing Temperatism that the idea of doing good isn't dismissed simply as something to be explored later, but also examined in regard to its basic premise upon which more meat can be added at a later date.

Meyer (2015) defines "doing good" as "undertaking actions to create a beneficial and sustainable situation for a company, the stakeholders and the community, the environment, and for society as a whole." The definition, arising from an exploration of positive business, examines how the fair distribution of wealth, "supporting ecologic and social justice" and ensuring that the wider community and natural environment flourish, is part of the equation of doing good (Meyer, 2015). Furthermore, treating employees fairly, with a strong emphasis on the development of wellbeing, inclusiveness, and sustainable work practices, is advocated as a way to develop a positive organizational system focused on improving long-term functioning both of the organization and of the society as a whole.

Another proposal or consideration for determining what constitutes "good" is offered by Skidelsky and Skidelsky (2010), who probably explain better than anything found in the research what a doing good Temperatist agenda might consist of in regard to their description of "'Basic Goods'— the goods that constitute living well. Health, respect, security, relationships of trust and love are recognized everywhere as part of a good human life; their absence is recognized everywhere as a misfortune." They go on to list and explain basic goods as including:

- *Health,* which relates to our physical and mental wellbeing and those things that relate to sustaining human life.
- *Security,* which relates to our expectations regarding our safety and protection.
- *Respect,* which relates to individual views and interests being treated as worthy of protection.
- *Personality,* which relates to autonomy for an individual to be who they are.
- *Harmony with nature,* which relates to reducing the external cost of human activities on the environment.
- *Friendship,* which relates to both personal and political union for the common good.
- *Leisure,* which relates to the opportunity to pursue activities or pursuits that have no other purpose than for our own sake, as well as time off from toil.

They also state that "although moral variety undoubtedly exists, it is less extensive than is often supposed . . . communalities define the distinctly human form of life" (Skidelsky and Skidelsky, 2010). Like an argument over what type of food dish is best, the output, that it is tasty, that it fills us up, that it satisfies us, is the same regardless of which dish you may promote as the best. Doing good in Temperatism can be defined by the outcome of an action, just as capitalism is focused on the profit outcome. However, unlike capitalism and the pursuit of profit, it is the *doing* in the doing good agenda that also covers the external costs of achieving the outcome, as requiring being *good* as well as the good result that is achieved.

Temperatism does not offer a utopian vision of what good looks like, beyond the protection of basic goods, that all human kind should be entitled to a minimum standard of living and an improvement must be made in regards to the distribution of wealth. This is different from previous socialist and communist attempts to introduce a doctrine of what utopia would look like. But as humanity, culture, and our environment change and adapt, our vision of what utopia could be would also shift. What was good in car design even 10 years ago is not the same as today. Temperatism does not advocate getting stuck on one form of doing good, since humanity does vary and does differ in its choices, hopes, dreams, and desires. But there are basic things that all humanity needs regardless of our culture, language, or country of birth. We also have within us, which capitalism has tried to deny, a capacity to do good and an underlying morality that goes beyond societal norms. Although capitalism has attempted to produce a system that is amoral, morality still impacts the market dependent on the strength of feeling and unity of society at any given moment.

Doing Good in Organizational Life

For too many years, organizations have been steadily marching to the beat of the capitalist drum. Finance and wealth creation has become gods, and humans have become the sacrificial lambs at the altar of shareholder's value and profit. The organization has within it the capacity to achieve the Plato ideal of devoting their purpose to that of public wellbeing. Corruption will still exist, mistakes will be made, and dishonesty will occur. Temperatism doesn't expect any organization to be perfect, and part of being human is that we have a capacity to make errors of judgment or take unnecessary risks. It is easy with hindsight to wish things were done differently or better. But the congruence and interdependency between economic, political, and social spheres supports the notion that no single entity has all the answers. Ideas about what doing good means will change over time, and as basic goods become the norm, our ideas regarding "minimum" standards of living will also increase. The difference is Temperatism demands that the truth of humanity's capacity and potential for doing good be released and freed from the shackles of monetization as a task.

In essence, Temperatism as an ideology advocates not just transforming but replacing the current capitalist market-led system and adopting a market system, which ensures that organizations and government have at their core a socially pursuant purpose and an ethical and values-driven agenda with performance measures composed of a primacy of societal measures rather than those that are purely financial. The desired result will be that doing good in regard to a socio-humanist context becomes the measure of success for organizations. This, however, does not mean that profit or the ownership of the means of production becomes transferred to the state or is owned by society as a whole. Instead, organizations and entrepreneurs will continue to be able to pursue business but in return will be restricted to an un-excessive and moderate return on investment that will be regulated only if necessary. What does this mean in practice? Individual property rights will still exist, but must be used in a balanced manner, with a purposeful pursuit of doing good in the wider social context. Profit can be made, but must not be the primary purpose of the organization or a result of a profit-centered self-interest.

This means that organizations become a people-centric environment where the true value of humanity, talent, inventiveness, and innovation is enjoyed for the good of all those within the organization and not just as a resource to be exploited. As people matter, people-first mind-set and approach to all decision-making will replace shareholder return and quarterly profit statements, which result in short-termism and represent the rising inequality of wealth distribution within the capitalist system. Profit share paid to shareholders has continued to rise steadily, while wage share has continued to decline. The results are a society out of balance. Is it right that shareholders get greater levels of return at a time when those working to produce value for the organization get such a low return on their effort that they can't afford to eat or pay their rent? Is the idiom of bleeding a stone dry over-zealous when discussing employee effort, remuneration, and shareholder return? If this disparity is not appropriate, then what is?

Temperatism is not adverse to shareholders receiving a profit share from the investment that they have made to a business, but under Temperatism, profit share would be a secondary objective after wage share in regard to distribution of surplus. However, Temperatism is concerned with more than just simple economics. Doing good covers a whole range of basic goods, so for employees as well as improved wages, there would be a requirement for organizations to improve the working conditions of their employees to an acceptable standard, including a restrained and sober approach to work–life balance—on the part of both the employee and the employer, as described by the basic good of leisure explored earlier.

Temperatism is not socialism; it rails against the idea that "the state" knows best and argues that state socialism is not the most efficient form of planning and decision-making. However, power in society must not reside in the hands of the tradition capitalist property owners. Instead social and communal agreement of what represents equable and fair distribution of wealth in regards to doing good would ensure that as well as organizations reducing income disparities and supporting the employee population in regard to training, education, and wellbeing, there is also a fair and equitable recognition of the investment return required for the owners of the means of production and the contribution organizations should make in regard to the wider societal good. Organizations should be supported to adopt a bottom-up rather than a leadership-focused approach to strategy and planning, reshaping command and control to a community-led movement. The question is what support is needed and in return for what?

One of the biggest issues that the UK will face in the next few years is possible power cuts and the continuing increasing disparity in access to energy. The current situation demonstrates the harm that short-term financial reporting and a profit agenda creates. The infrastructure required to deliver an adequate response to the energy crisis in the UK requires a large upfront capital investment with return over decades. In the context of capitalism there is little incentive for energy companies, who are posting large profit figures, to seek to invest heavily in the infrastructure when it will have a significant impact on their bottom-line profit not just this year but for years to come.

The fact that the energy companies will receive a return on that investment over a period of 50 years is of no comfort to the shareholders or the

CEOs of the energy companies today and is not in their interests now, when the investment should be being made. The alternative energy proposals are costly and the cost of producing "green energy" is significantly more than fossil fuels, therefore making margins smaller. At the same time, the energy companies or organizations who use large percentages of the energy supply don't want to pay additional taxes, which would be needed if the government were to commit to building the infrastructure themselves. Quite frankly, the situation is that the energy companies want their cake of profit today and they want to eat it by getting the "government" (read taxpayer) to pay for the capital infrastructure upon which they will make their profits tomorrow. All the while, the organizations want to reduce the level of tax they are paying.

A Temperatist approach would seek to involve a partnership between government and energy companies paying for and keeping up to a high standard the infrastructure needed for energy production. If energy companies want to "sell" energy, they need to make it here, and they need to do so in a way that will have a reductionist impact on the environment. It is not as insane as it sounds to suggest that it should be organizations who should make the decisions in regard to investment, even in the context of the previous critique of organizational motivations. The government does not have the capacity to innovate and invent the processes and infrastructure needed for such a challenge, and the people best placed for delivering efficient energy supply in the UK are the organizations that have an interest in producing energy efficiently.

Big energy companies may choose to take their ball home, if required to invest heavily for the long term. They may even threaten to leave if regulatory frameworks affect their short-term profit measures. But we should not fear ultimatums because where a void in the market is created, entrepreneurs will fill the space. That is why Temperatism isn't a socialist or communist movement. The market is a great mechanism for innovation, advancement, and wealth creation. Temperatism doesn't want to throw the baby out with the bathwater. But doing good has to come before profits. So yes, an organization needs to make profits to survive and make a contribution in order for good to be an achievable outcome. The government has a role to play in supporting large public projects in regards to planning agreements protecting investment in public infrastructure and where appropriate with tax relief or government sponsorship to support organizations, which are taking big risks. But under Temperatism, an organization posting large profits at a time when the infrastructure is failing and societal good is threatened would not be tolerated, because in this situation, as today, profits are being put ahead of doing good and, even worse, mortgaging the future long-term sustainability of the organizations to produce a shareholder return today. The current system allows profits to get in the way of our progress, security, and societal sustainability. Therefore, Temperatism challenges the primacy of shareholder return ahead of the rights of society as a whole.

Temperatism is therefore maternalistic, but it is not socialist or communist in its construction. Regulation is important, but only insofar as ensuring that doing good is applied equitably to all in society. The government must and should protect the rights and lives of those they are called to serve; this means that the government, regardless of politics, is always on the side of society as a whole, never any one group or individual. Like capitalism, Temperatism will reward those who innovate and there will be an emphasis on encouraging innovation and investment in new ideas. Furthermore, improvements in efficiency and effectiveness will be supported and change encouraged in the never-ending pursuit of doing good. There is no restriction to what good looks like or what good can be achieved. The only limit is our imagination.

Orthodoxy and Doctrine

Of obvious concern is that the idea that doing good becomes a political doctrine or a religious orthodoxy, which rather than improving the lives of humanity oppresses it. There are plenty of moral conundrums in society, such as abortion, and enough historical evidence even in the last century that demonstrates that good can be twisted to incite hatred and harm to others. Once again, the emphasis on the basic goods must be the center stage. Whether or not you agree with someone's choices of lifestyle is not for Temperatism to decide. Like capitalism there is freedom of choice in regard to how you live your life. The proviso, of course, is that it should not impinge on the freedom of other people to live their lives, or on the societal norms of basic goods as outlined previously. Constitutional protections are important in this arena and many already exist, but it will be the regulation of the market in regard to the purpose of organizations in society that will bring the biggest protests and have the most dramatic effect. Temperatism is in effect a planned market economy in that it continues to support the market economy as long as it supports the societal goal of doing good. The ideology does not support government planning, because it would simply transfer wealth distribution from the power of the market to the political power of the day.

Creating a societal culture where doing good for the wider social context is considered more important than individual self-interest and rewards and encouragement for placing society interest above the need to consume will be in the hands of the government and organizations. Enjoying the good life and enjoying material things shouldn't be the be all and end all of our culture. There is nothing wrong with an extra pair of shoes or a new gadget that makes your life easier or more enjoyable, but they should no longer be the driving force of our lives. The commercialization of Christmas is a contemporary example of a shift that needs to be reversed.

Christmas used to be about family time. Gifts were exchanged, but were not the central part of the holiday. The pressure on families now begins as early as September. Christmas displays in shops, with all that glitters and plastic that buzzes and beeps, arrive before the kids have returned to school from their summer holidays. Twenty-five percent of the year is devoted to selling consumers stuff that they neither really want, nor probably, almost definitely don't need. Parents who both work full-time to keep up with their consumer life style are made to feel guilty if they don't buy their children the latest fashion or toy craze, all of which cost hundreds of pounds. Christmas has become a festival to the consumer culture and that culture is being passed onto the next generation. Is this how we wish to live our lives? Is this the purpose of our time on earth, to consume at greater and greater levels until we die? Is that all that a human life can or indeed should represent? Temperatism isn't a doctrine that declares material goods as being bad, but that the pursuit of materialism and the place that consumerism has in our society is no longer good for us. Like the role of alcohol in an alcoholic's life, it is not that alcohol is necessarily a bad thing, but that it needs to be taken in moderation to avoid it being "bad." Material goods are the same. A little bit of what you fancy never does any harm, but what is preventing working hours from falling, driving criminals to pursue crime, and leading to alienation and societal breakdown is too much of a good thing, and the things we are pursuing contribute to unhappiness rather than improving the quality of our lives. Temperatism doesn't hate wealth, but it does seek to change our relationship with wealth, to question the purpose of wealth in our society, and to pursue a purpose for the wealth that we create that is good. Most of all, Temperatism wants to make sure that we all benefit, equitably, if not equally from the possibilities that wealth offers.

Impossibly Possible Endeavors

I write the above knowing that many people will argue that Temperatism is idealism and that we can't change the economic, social, or political system. My response is to remind people that societal shifts are possible. William Wilberforce and the abolition campaigners ended 200 years of British involvement in the transatlantic slave trade. The impossible is possible. Tolstoy observed that it is "an infinitely large number of infinitesimally small actions" that make us all potential history makers. Temperatism is based on the whole of society all working together, all pulling together in one direction. It becomes possible in the first place through a joint endeavor, and its very continuance relies on each and every one of us doing good in small ways, as well as collectively delivering doing good in an organized way to be possible or successful.

Consider for a moment the well of kindness that resides in all of humanity. Think of the last time that you experienced a random act of kindness that completely changed the situation in which you found yourself. It might have been someone offering you a seat on a crowded train, someone returning something that you had been unaware you had dropped, a helping hand or a more substantial gift of generosity that was game changing to your circumstances at the time. Notice how those random acts of kindness all happened at a time when you were in need, when you were lacking and someone else stepped in to fill the gap. Temperatism isn't based on cloud cuckoo land thinking. It is a reflection of something that happens in every part of the world, every single day, and is increasingly present in our consciousness. It is a scaling-up of those opportunities we experience when we allow ourselves to give and receive Good.

The moment I began to think such a thing was possible was during the London Olympics 2012, which demonstrated our ability as a society to pull together, and the resulting "high" we felt as we discovered we were part of something bigger. As well as a celebration of the brilliant sporting achievements of all the athletes regardless of which nation they represented, it was the volunteer game makers who were applauded for their efforts in connecting with visitors and helping to make their experience a good one. The result was an atmosphere that was like no other. It felt good to be part of something where people were doing good. It is true that humanity is imperfect and we all have the ability to do bad things to each other and to get it wrong. But Temperatism is based on the belief that inside each individual is the ability to do ordinary things extraordinarily well and that we all possess an in-built desire to do Good.

The Economic Agenda Is Not Inevitable

The good news is that we are not subject to the whims and whimsy of those who are currently in power. They only have power, because we as a collective allow them to retain it. The 1998 Disney Pixar film *Bugs Life* may seem like a strange place to draw inspiration for societal reform, but there is one line in there that serves the purpose of reminding us all what we are capable of: "Ants are not meant to serve grasshoppers. I've seen these ants do great things and year after year, they somehow manage to pick enough food for themselves and you. So-so who's the weaker species? Ants don't serve grasshoppers! It's you who need us! We're a lot stronger than you say we are. And you know it, don't you?" The financiers in the city, the CEO, the political leaders, they all allow us to do extraordinary things year after year. They take our inventiveness, innovation, abilities, talent, and hard work and exploit it for their own ends. Society doesn't serve the market, or the government; they need us and we are all a lot more valuable and stronger than we have been led to believe. It is time to break free of the shackles of capitalism and demand a future worthy of humanity.

In their book *How Much Is Enough?* Skidelsky and Skidelsky write, "Making money cannot be an end in itself . . . And what is true of individuals is also true of societies. Making money cannot be the permanent business of humanity" (Skidelsky and Skidelsky, 2012). Cunningham goes on, "The human being is more than an economic being; we are social, aesthetic, cultural, sexual beings and we have many selves, many intelligences and many rationalities. There is more to life than work that has been commoditized and defined by commodities" (Cunningham, 2004). A core belief of Temperatism is that human beings are *more than*, that is at its heart Temperatism is a new way to think about business which is rooted in an old idea, the socio-humanist pursuit of the meaning of life; the belief that at work and at play people are more than machines or consumers and are socially interdependent.

Temperatism argues that the pursuit of the current market-led system by organizations and governments is fundamentally flawed in delivering effectiveness and long-term value and releasing the potential of the wider human community, as well as damaging the future prosperity of the human race by encouraging "the view that our natural environment is merely a factor of production from which maximum utility is to be squeezed, rather than accepting that as a species we are no more than part of the complex ecosystem" (Hart, 1993). It questions whether the managerial, strategic, and control-focused approaches to organizations and government are the only option available to humanity.

Temperatism suggests that the economic agenda is not inevitable, although many assume it is. Organizations have the capacity to be a force for good in our society. The philanthropic pursuits of individuals—such as the Lever brothers, who built Port Sunlight; the cooperative nature of John Lewis; the work of charities; and the voluntary, community, and not-for-profit sector—and the pursuit of corporate social responsibility may not be perfect, but all demonstrate that a different agenda is possible. The human race has a large capability to be flexible and adapt to the environment in which we find ourselves. As problem solvers and improvers, we are restless in our pursuit of betterment. At times, such as these when we find ourselves stuck in a hole, we challenge our thinking and our assumptions until eventually a new imagining of what is possible emerges and the old ways fall away.

Temperatism does not advocate that scarce resources and organizations should be owned or controlled by the community as in socialism or by the state as in communism. The history of these ideologies appears to lead to other inequalities, namely, in regard to power and corruption. "Communism was seen as modernity's main model of opposition to capitalist economic and social organisation, but it falls into the trap of outlining a society in which man is not seen as an individual anymore, but as a commodity whose labour is bought and sold on the markets" (Suciu, 2009).

Temperatism argues that the owners of production should receive benefit for the risks they take and leaders rewarded for good stewardship, delivering sustainable performance that secures jobs and improves the lives and wellbeing of employees. But when profits aren't being made and largesse of pay still exists and the gap between employee and senior management pay continues to grow while employees struggle to put food on the table, then the balance between reward and effort has gone wrong. Rather Temperatism promotes a more temperate approach to the means of production, distribution, and the exchange of wealth and, most importantly, the human condition. It advocates a more calm and moderate approach to economic, social, and political efforts and a focus on doing good. What Temperatism is not is a social form of capitalism, or a synthesis of some of the more moderate forms of socialism and capitalism. Instead, it promotes an economic system that has at its center an ethical, moral, and values-driven approach, which can "be a positive and productive force in society, it should not be the only (nor even the most important) influence on societal values" (Hart, 1993). Temperatism advocates an agenda, where doing something because it is the right thing to do provides a nonnegotiable moral compass in both organizational and government decision-making.

What would it take for organizations and government to pursue a genuinely ethical and values-driven agenda? What if organizational purpose was not ultimately about delivering shareholder value but about furthering the health and wellbeing in society? Should society exclude economic and political activity that does not build community and do good in the wider societal context?

Temperatism proposes that the biggest challenge our world faces is not the ending of the pursuit of profit, greed, self-interest, criminal activity, slavery, child abuse, violence, or any of the hundreds of violations and hurts that humans have the capacity to inflict on each other and our planet, although these are all issues that are important and need tackling. Rather it will argue that the biggest issue facing the world today is simply the lack of doing good because we have been believing it is a viable outcome.

CHAPTER 6

More Than Capitalism with a Heart

The be-all and end-all of life should not be to get rich, but to enrich the world.

—B. C. Forbes

Temperatism is more than a bleeding heart version of the capitalist ideal. Its purpose is to tackle key injustices and social inequality that are symptoms of the capitalist market system. By focusing on an agenda of doing good, Temperatism seeks to reduce the level of elitism and social exclusion, that capitalism claims are inevitable, by sharing access to resources and ensuring that all individuals have the opportunity to exercise their talent potential. Furthermore, it aims to tackle despair head on through the pursuit and delivery of basic goods and make a declaration that humanity has the ability to pursue betterment for all. Lastly, through a demonstration of temperance in regard to social responsibility of enoughness, Temperatism aims to challenge prejudices based on wealth distortion. At the same time, the new way to think about business aims to highlight the societal benefit of wealth creation or profit with a purpose and counteract the damage that the enrichment of the wealthy few at the expense of the majority has on longer term sustainability. The "trickle down" effect is not efficient; it is wasteful of human potential. Allowing small percentages of individuals to be fabulously rich while others die of hunger, thirst, and easily treatable diseases is based on corrupt thinking, made worse by the acceptance that the fabulously rich are normal in trying to avoid proportionality in supporting society through taxation. For change to happen, it is necessary for the growing noise of opposition regarding the social make-up of our society to be heard but not succumbing to the destructive tendencies of the populist mob. In history there are plenty of examples of shifts in acceptance of injustice, whether in the realization that racial segregation, homophobia, or attitudes toward women are abhorrent; humanity continually demonstrates its ability to mature in its continuum of doing good. The capability of humanity to challenge normalcy and declare what was once acceptable as unacceptable is what brings hope that an alternative to capitalism is possible.

For Temperatism to become reality, a society-wide cultural shift would need to take place. The growing body of work, which has increased inexorably since the credit crunch, suggests that there are many, whether in academia or in the public media, who are questioning the profit motive that drives capitalism and are deeply mistrustful of the concept of perpetual growth, which is an imperative of the capitalist system and leads to the question as to whether a moderate or sustainable capitalism is, in fact, possible. These concerns go against the grain for economists who see no alternative to the capitalist agenda who actively disparage any attempt to question a rationality that has been developed over many decades and embedded itself into Western culture and attitudes. However, the rise in reactionary populist movements demonstrates that the time for new thinking is now, if progression rather than regression is to be our future.

Temperatism makes no apology for taking the disturbing truth about our economic system and placing it in the harsh light of reality, and on reflection it provides uncomfortable viewing. Currently, society makes excuses and creates deniability of the brutal truth; capitalism is harming our society, harming the planet, and harming humanity. We try to convince ourselves that capitalism isn't wrong per se; it just needs adjusting, resulting in considerations of new ways of working and suggestions of sustainable, social, moderate, or responsible capitalism. "'The idea of an all-powerful market without any rules and any political intervention is mad,' said Nicolas Sarkozy, adding that 'Self-regulation is finished. Laissez faire is finished.' Henry Paulson, the U.S. Treasury Secretary agreed: 'Raw capitalism is a dead end'" (Naim, 2008). Think-tanks have been searching for a new paradigm to replace the attitudes and behaviors that lead to the credit crunch. What was, is no longer possible or permissible, but what replaces what was, is yet to be decided. However, we don't like to admit the truth, that we, the West, have got it wrong. Having beaten socialism and communism, becoming the hero of democracy, and developing a model others want to copy, we can't bring ourselves to say capitalism wasn't such a great idea either. We're not ready or willing to eat humble pie just yet.

The issue, however, isn't a debate about who owns the means of production, or whether the laissez-faire market model is good or bad for human society. Instead the issue at the heart of the debate is focused on the rights and wrongs of capitalism as an economic model and the resulting short-term and profit-motivated thinking in Western business, what Chris Grey has called fast capitalism. Short-term, quarterly results–focused thinking is bad for business, it is bad for people, and it is bad for society. What is clear is that it is time for change. The capitalist system isn't working. The business cycle doesn't protect the vulnerable, but it contributes to a system where more people are made vulnerable because of the inequality of reward and brutalization of the workplace. There is no security, even for those who do work, and for those who cannot get work there is a greater level of insecurity than before the abolition of the workhouse during the Victorian era.

Focusing on the Human Element

Rather than blame the weaknesses in the system, the blame for homelessness or domestic financial problems is that the individual who is poor is in that situation because they have not worked or are not working hard enough. In the capitalist system it is the individual who lacks the aspiration and motivation and makes poor lifestyle choices, usually in the form of drinking alcohol or smoking, which means that they cannot afford to keep a roof over their head or food on the table. "*Why should we,*" the utilitarian economist will ask, "*pay to help others who refuse to help themselves?*" In this framing, the poor are not deserving of help, because the capitalist system supposes that it provides the means by which each individual is able to help themselves, and if society were to provide for those who can't provide for themselves, the result is the creation of a system that encourages people to continue to be lazy and feckless. But this attitude is based on false assumptions. A report by the Joseph Rowntree Foundation in 2015 shows that 6.8 million people who are in a working family in the UK are living in poverty and that in-work poverty now outstrips out-of-work poverty. This isn't feckless, work shy, individuals, but people who are working hard and still struggling to have their basic needs met. As the pay gap between those at the top and those at the bottom widen, you have to ask the question whether those selling their labor are getting a proportional share of the value created by organizations. It is this lack of heart that is most disturbing in the capitalist system. The ability to lay blame and assume guilt on the guiltless is both disturbing and unhelpful in providing the means to solve issues such as poverty and social deprivation.

The enterprise culture forgets that human capital has a human element to it and people feel powerless to try and change anything, so 60 percent of us are in a job we hate. What a waste! A fundamental belief at the center of Temperatism is that we are all of equal worth, we all have value to add and potential to release, and we are equally important in regard to having our basic goods provided for. We all deserve security, health, friendship, etc. for no other reason than we are human. For those who are struggling, it is their circumstances that define their ability to change. Being born with the proverbial silver spoon in your mouth is as much an accident of birth as being born into poverty. Temperatism isn't about blame, but a willingness to accept that wealth is not necessarily a result of discretionary effort and those who have good luck should take responsibility to defend those who find themselves victims of bad luck. In the UK there is a fondness for the NHS because we believe that it is the defining feature of the society we wish to be part of, where access to good healthcare is an inalienable human right. We are willing to support such measures through taxation because we believe in its inherent goodness. But fear of exploitation in areas such as poverty alleviation are more complicated, because we have been led to believe that poverty is the due dessert for failing to work hard. For many, circumstances beyond their control can lead them to be victims, unable to fulfill their potential or promise because something has got in their way. It may be illness, change, or loss that causes someone to be a victim rather than a conqueror. In the right environment we all have the ability to flourish and do well. We all have the capacity to be creative and innovative. But sometimes life throws us a curve ball that we aren't expecting and that can damage our ability to look after ourselves. It is for these circumstances that Temperatism proposes we must develop a heart that says society is here to catch you. For some circumstances it might be a national disaster, caused by natural phenomenon such as earthquakes, hurricanes, flooding, or droughts; for individuals, circumstances such as illness, loss, or change can deliver a blow to their ability to reach their potential.

It is the interpretation of fault that centers Temperatism. Though some decisions made by individuals within poverty are incomprehensible because they make the situation worse rather than better, the assumption must be that these bad decisions are an exception rather than a rule. To paint everyone with a brush, which says that if you are poor, it is your fault for not taking the opportunities available to you, fails to understand the inequalities and deep-rooted unfairness in society, which keeps the poor, poor and lays blame at the door of the wrong people.

Short-Term Growth Versus the Human Heart

The focus of organizations and the economic system in which they participate has become so short term that the long-term measures that benefit both people and the sustainability of organizations are lost. Investing in skills and developing people's potential is ignored because people become little more than a variable cost on the balance sheet. Temperatism advocates that the value that a person can bring is so much more than something that comes out of a box. But to understand anything of true value requires an environment that gives space for people to unlock their potential. One writer, Kenneth Rogoff (2006), argues that

none of capitalism's problems is insurmountable and economists have offered a variety of market-based solutions. A high global price for carbon would induce firms and individuals to internalize the cost of their polluting activities. Tax systems can be designed to provide a measure of redistribution of income without necessarily involving crippling distortions, by minimizing non-transparent tax expenditures and keeping marginal rates low. Effective pricing of health care, including the pricing of waiting times, could encourage a better balance between equality and efficiency.

Financial systems could be better regulated, with stricter attention to excessive accumulations of debt. (Rogoff, 2006)

Even if it were possible that all these things could happen, and the likelihood of that is slim, fundamentally the profit agenda, which is the primary objective, prevents capitalism from being an economic system that has humanity at its heart. The economic and social problems we are experiencing is because capitalism doesn't work, even in a mixed market economy. Without government intervention social good will always be at the mercy of self-interest and capitalism will do whatever it can to avoid or reduce regulation.

Ironically, the events of 2008 meant that the capitalist economic system was on the verge of collapse and the only thing that saved it was government intervention. The market was bailed out by the state and European governments are struggling with the consequences of what should have been capitalism's last big bust. Though the market would like the public to believe that it is back to business as usual, the truth is that nations are still pumping money into the system to try to get the market engine running properly. The world remains out of balance, the market has not been restored, merely propped up and yet the pursuit of a profit agenda and growth continues as if nothing had changed. In many ways, part of the problem is that we can't quite believe that capitalism is broken. Our self-delusion leaves us searching in the rubble for an economic answer that has already self-combusted. Capitalism has wormed its way into our psyche and we are not quite ready to let it go.

We are told time and again by those in charge of our economies that we need to grow but the end game of growth might not be the outcome that we are looking for.

Certainly growth of a certain kind would increase well-being in large parts of the planet—increased access to healthy food, clean water, effective waste disposal, health care, education and to employment. But do we have any good reason that capitalist growth will provide these things? Certainly the historical record suggests the contrary . . . Indeed, capitalism's desperate drive to grow is deeply implicated in the persistence of global poverty. (Schweickart, 2009)

Temperatism would argue that make do and mend is not the way to a brighter future and restoring something that is so toxic to our wellbeing would result in future generations experiencing greater extremes of boom and bust and either the system is destroyed or we are.

At its center Temperatism seeks to get to the heart of humanity. Capitalism doesn't care, and it doesn't care that it doesn't care. But as human beings we should care. We should care about the fact that we are currently subjected to the whims of an economic system that has no heart, has no meaning beyond profit, and diminishes humanity to numbers and statistics. We should value human life. But we have become immune to the charity advertisements on television that plead with us to part with a small contribution every month to help provide clean water, education, healthcare, and food to those in need. We can look at the problems in our society and feel helpless to be able to know where to start to solve them. We can, as the capitalists do, make excuses that there will always be poor, unemployed, homeless, and the disenfranchised. We can ignore the difficulties in the contrast between the haves and have-nots and close our door at night. Or we can make a different decision. We can allow ourselves to feel again, to let our hearts break for the broken, but more importantly, we can look in the mirror, search our hearts, and realize that we are just the man or woman to do something about it. If enough of us, Malcolm Gladwell suggests 150 people, decide that something has to be different, that we must listen to the call of our heart and stop ignoring the pain that we see, then maybe Temperatism can become a new way to think about business and doing good.

By reducing us to self-interested individuals, capitalism denies our humanity and our ability to wield a social power and community spirit that can move mountains (sometimes quite literally) and produce powerful results. Together humans are greater than the sum of our parts. Temperatism is about building up and empowering the separated and weakened individualism of the capitalist system to join individuals together to be a united force for change and doing good. Humanity is not just a species that dominates planet Earth; it is more than that; humanity is a type of moral character that we all have in common. To pretend that businesses are amoral, that organizational leaders don't have to decide between good and bad, that it is possible to run organizations unaffected by the consequences of our actions upon others, is to deny that organizations are by their very nature human, with a heart and spirited nature. We can't stop being human. We can't stop having a heart.

Adopting a Human Agenda

Temperatism isn't thinking small, nor am I naïve as to what it would take to make the change: thousands of people and a majority of business leaders deciding to think differently. Whole systems would need to change, albeit changing something that is broken is easier than changing something that is working. Moreover, asking individuals to be more of what they are, rather than continuing to be what they are not, is an easier agenda than the reverse. Moving an organization and government from a capitalist profit agenda to a Temperatist agenda would require a move from a 'greed is good' mentality and embracing a moderate and self-restrained platform based on a long-term commitment to the common good, abstinence from overindulgence, community-based programs, and the use of human creativity and innovation to produce economically viable ways of bettering all. Such an agenda, so easily written on the pages of a book, requires a shift from self-interest to social interest and that requires humans to get back in touch with their humanity, to accept responsibility and hold each other accountable. Not exactly an agenda that would get the voters to vote for someone during an election. Or is it?

But there are plenty of reasons why individuals might choose to change their habits and be part of a Temperatist culture. In his book *Why Capitalism?* Allan Meltzer begins by declaring that capitalism as a system is successful because of its "foundation of a rule of law, which protects individual rights to property and, in the first instance, aligns rewards to values produced. Working hand in hand with the rule of law, capitalism gives its participants incentives to act as society desires, typically rewarding hard work, intelligence, persistence and innovation" (Meltzer, 2012). This view of capitalism rewarding effort is in line with the traditional view of the American Dream, the opportunity for anyone to make good if they work hard enough. However, it is the realization that hard work doesn't get rewarded that is driving the current swell of populism. Although capitalism has delivered some improvements in regard to efficiency and the innovations and inventiveness of man has been spurred by the opportunity for personal gain and the possibility of wealth, capitalism creates a conflict between the pursuit for the efficient use of resources and the effectiveness of those resources being used to create an equitable reward for individual effort. Furthermore, the financial reward incentive clashes with the desire of individuals for greater meaning to our lives and the in-built fairness node that needs an intrinsic value to human life. The focus on efficiency places an emphasis on doing things right even if the things that are being done are rational but wrong, or more specifically immoral. The uncomfortable feeling that occurs when business decisions are made, that sit uneasy on the shoulders of those burdened with the implementation of a business plan, is what is at the center of who we are as humans. Temperatism pursues effectiveness first, pursuing a course of action that ensures that government, organizations, and society are focused on doing the right things, doing good first and foremost.

CHAPTER 7

Property and Employment

As soon as the land of any country has become private property, the landlords, like all other men, love to reap where they never sowed, and demand rent event for its natural produce.

—Adam Smith

One area that cannot remain unaddressed is the area of property rights. The capitalist economy is built on the back of the right to own property and the unequal distribution of resources. The gap between those who have property and those who don't is at the center of the inequality that divides our society. Under capitalism those who do not own property or material resources find themselves outside of the protection of the custodian of capitalism, the rule of law, and any protection that the amoral rule of law might provide to their individual rights. Pressure from government and society is heeded only when it becomes impossible to ignore and if regulation is imposed. But the more powerful the capitalist elite becomes, the more disenfranchised individuals become, and even Meltzer (2012) confirms that the actors in a capitalist system will find ways to circumvent the rules that prevent the market from doing what it wants anyway. Those who have property, it appears, are therefore able to get away with more than those who don't.

The capitalist system promotes property rights; in the UK and the United States, through privatization people have been encouraged to buy shares in public utilities, and owning your own home has been promoted through the relaxation of mortgage-lending rules. In the UK, in the 1980s the Thatcher government unleashed the property-owning instincts of capitalism through enabling those who were in social housing the right to buy. Under the magnifying glass of Temperatism it could be argued that the Thatcher government was doing good by allowing those who were renting property to become property owners themselves. It also removed the burden of the local government housing stock from being a cost to the taxpayer to that of individual owners. We could, of course, with 20:20 vision criticize that decision in regard to the fact that the UK now suffers from a social housing shortage, the bursting of the housing bubble in the 1990s, and the toxic debts and subprime mortgage lending that led to the credit crunch.

If we consider the right to buy from a social interest rather than a self-interest perspective, the dynamics of the rightness of the policy from a Temperatist perspective shifts somewhat. The purpose of social housing was to provide a home for those in crisis, for the roofless, so the greatest good in regard to Temperatism wasn't to increase the property ownership of those already in accommodation but to ensure the protection of those who were most in need and without accommodation. This demonstrates a subtle but significant difference that affects decision-making when it comes to the possibilities of two goods. By selling off social housing, the Thatcher government increased the wealth of those already housed, but at the cost of reducing the help available to those who were not housed at all. As a consequence, the gap between the haves and the have-nots was increased. This is borne out by statistics that shows that from the 1980s until 2003 there was an upward trend in the number of households that were counted as unintentionally homeless and a similar trend in regard to the number of people housed in temporary accommodation (Joseph Rowntree Foundation, 2012). Improvements from 2003 correspond with the introduction of the public sector Homelessness Strategy, although part of that strategy was to change the way homelessness was assessed, dramatically reducing the number who were now classed as homeless without changing the numbers in situations that would be previously have been classed as homeless. A recent report showed that homelessness in England increased by 32 percent from 2009/2010 to 2015/2016, and 64 percent of local authorities surveyed are struggling to find social tenancies for homeless people (Joseph Rowntree Foundation, 2017). In the UK the right to buy is back on the agenda, and homelessness continues to be a growing problem. The outcome of tax and benefit reform focused on extending property rights has resulted in moving the UK from being one of the most equal societies in Europe to being one with the greatest level of inequality in less than 20 years.

Since the 1980s, the ups and downs of the housing market has become a mainstay of Western domestic finances and directly impacts on the business climate. However, it was the heady pursuit of home ownership and the subprime mortgage market that directly contributed to the financial crash and credit crunch in 2008. Therefore, it could be argued that property rights directly affect the fortunes of organizations as well as the wellbeing of their employees. The very survival of Western economies was threatened because financial corporations had played a game of poker with ever more complex trades and increasing opaqueness regarding the vast quantities of toxic debt the institutions were exposed to. Not only were the legal boundaries of credit lending, especially around the subprime mortgage market, stretched beyond its limits, so too was the morality of the institutions involved in regard to both their decision to lend to those who were never in a position to repay what they were borrowing and their deliberate evasion of regulatory propriety and ultimately the legality of their operations. The resulting credit crunch directly impacted on the ability of businesses to engage in regular financing of their business operations, causing many viable businesses to hit the wall.

Furthermore, the resulting debt burden caused by the push for greater levels of property ownership has affected those at the lower end of the income scale the most. Unable to keep up with mortgage payments, many have lost their home and the security of a roof over their head. This is a painful place to be and injurious to the wellbeing of individuals in that situation. The rising levels of stress, depression, and anxiety demonstrate that home ownership, rather than being a blessing, has become a curse. However, the mixture of low interest rates and the increasing price of rental property because of the house price boom and housing shortages means that many rentals now exceed the affordability of the average worker, thus removing the basic need for secure housing. Having created a bubble and removed the safety net, the response to the housing crisis and the resulting poverty has not met with sympathy by the capitalist cultural mind-set.

Digital Property

Questions regarding the equality of property ownership have also begun to stretch beyond that of the traditional ideas of corporate shareholding and property. In September 2012, a story appeared claiming that Actor Brue Willis was suing Apple for the right to pass on his iTunes library to his children; although the story about Willis and his music collection turned out to be untrue, it did bring the subject of who owns digital downloads to the public's attention. This goes beyond "what is mine, is mine" into the territory of "and what is yours is mine too." Since 2001, consumers have been downloading digital music, paying for a music collection that could be played on their MP4 players, and enjoying the portability of their music collections wherever they go. However, like many who purchase goods online, the majority failed to read the terms and conditions of the download service. Now consumers have begun to realize that they have been buying digital music in the same way that they bought CDs and Vinyl, believing that if the downloads were legal then the collection of music and film became their property, which is an asset that is theirs to sell or pass on if they choose. However, it turns out, if you read the small print, the music or digital book download is a loan and it can't be passed onto relatives or friends when we die. It has no value beyond our own use—digital downloads are no more than a lifetime loan from a lending library belonging to the organization we bought it from, not us. Digital music and eBooks can't be resold in the same way that past generations resold their physical music collections or old books; there will no longer be second-hand music shops or books sellers, nor piles of unwanted media filling the shelves of charity shops. You can listen to the music as much as you like, you can read and reread the books as many times as you choose on your digital devices, but you can't pass it on to your children or even bestow the unwanted items to charity shops. The price that consumers are paying for digital down-loads is the price of a personal lifetime lending fee. For the consumer, the gadgets offered the opportunity of flexibility and meant that they could read any book in their personal library or listen to any song in their music collection wherever they were in the world. What consumers have now discovered is that they have bought into the world's biggest library-lending scheme; their digital property is nothing more than an illusion of ownership.

In a market system where property rights are sacrosanct and part of the rule of law, it is interesting that the biggest consumer revolution of the last decade has ensured that the property rights have remained in the hands of the organizations who are selling what the consumer thought was a product, but what has turned out to be little more than a service. Furthermore, consumers can lose access to their legally purchased collections if their digital library providers decide that they have violated the terms of their account, which, if you have ever tried to read the terms and conditions, is buried in a myriad of legal contract terms that you need a legal degree to decipher and, unlike normal consumer rights, fails to provide a mechanism by which the consumer has the right of appeal or explanation. The digital media consumers download is no more tangible than a haircut they had six months ago. There is no doubt that as the realization dawns on the consumer, legal challenges and the regulatory framework regarding digital property rights will catch up and the terms and conditions will change or at least become more transparent. But when ownership becomes an illusion, the question has to be asked as to whether the market system and big business are looking to deliver freedom and democracy or more ingenious ways to retain property rights for themselves.

The Asset Rich and Asset Poor

Despite a growth in property and share ownership since the 1980s, there is still a large disparity between those who have assets and those who do not. "The poorest quarter of Britain's population owns less than 1 per cent of the nation's assets, while the top 3 per cent own a sixth. This equates to roughly 1.5 million people owning assets worth £1 trillion" (Hutton, 2011). Therefore, the distribution of assets in society demonstrates the inequality that capitalism generates. Inheritance and wealth taxes are a contentious issue, but one that must be tackled if Temperatism is to be successful. Those who have built up a property empire, or are asset rich, would probably feel aggrieved that the wealth that *they* have generated should go toward helping the disadvantaged, used in socially responsible projects, or be redistributed for the purpose of creating greater levels of equality. The American Dream is based on the theory that you can start from nothing and make it, and it is true that there are many rags-to-riches stories available for us to marvel over. But for every person who is living the dream, there are millions who haven't made it because the circumstances of birth have not afforded him or her the opportunities that the very wealthy have the privilege of receiving. Monboit (2016) suggests that "the rich persuade themselves that they acquired their wealth through merit, ignoring the advantages—such as education, inheritance and class—that may have helped to secure it. The poor begin to blame themselves for their failures, even when they can do little to change their circumstances." You only have to listen to President Trump declare himself a self-made man and nonchalant references to a "small" $14 million loan from his father to understand how perceptions of wealth generation differ depending on your experience of wealth.

The UK Labour Party's fight with Oxbridge about setting a percentage of placements to those children from a lower social background was indicative of the leg-up that existing wealth affords. Whatever measures that you choose, if you come from a wealthy background, you are more likely to be wealthy, to have wealth, and to be in a position of power. Devising a mechanism for wealth or asset redistribution to ensure that proportional equity is achieved is not the same as a socialist or communist pursuit of everyone being the same, but a simple recognition that those who have, have a responsibility to contribute more than those who have not, because the very fact that you have makes it easier for you to get more. For those who are born in wealthy circumstances, it is as simple as if they have the privilege of a 13-mile head start in a marathon. Not only is it more likely that they will finish first, but for those who have to run the full marathon, finishing the race takes a lot more effort. For the poorest in the world the race is even harder.

This is even more apparent when we consider the difference between the wealthy West and third world countries.

> The poor bear responsibility for too many aspects of their lives. The richer you are, the more the "right" decisions are made for you. The poor have no piped water and therefore do not benefit

from the chlorine that the city government puts into the water supply. If they want clean drinking water, they have to purify it themselves. They cannot afford ready-made fortified breakfast cereals and therefore have to make sure that they and their children get enough nutrients. They have no automatic way to save, such as a retirement plan or a contribution to Social Security, so they have to make sure that they save . . . For the poor . . . their lives are already much more demanding than ours. (Banerjee and Duflo, 2011)

The capitalist mentality of "what is mine is mine" is selfish and unfair because it denies the reality of a privileged position that a headstart affords and the advantages that the wealthy have. The inequality between the wealthy and the not wealthy in regard to the opportunities available is detrimental to the ongoing success of human society, because it never allows the poor to catch up, so poverty and wealth are as a result of the failures and successes of previous generations repeated in a pattern of opportunity and luck according to an accident of birth.

Resolving Unemployment

The conferring of status through the ownership of material resources and property has a devastating effect on the human condition if those things are lost or reduced. Since we are no longer valued for who we are, but what we have, the loss of status goods reduces a person both in their own mind and in the mind of society. This belief might seem odd to begin with. Of course, we don't judge people and think they are less of a person because they have lost their material wealth, most of us aren't that shallow. But there is an underlying belief that those that are in poverty, whether in our own society or in third world countries, are somehow less worthy of support and less worthy of our time and effort, and are lacking in value because they lack the means to support themselves. No one would admit that they see the homeless as less than themselves, but we cross the street to avoid them and sneer in contempt at the way in which *they* have allowed themselves to fall from being socially acceptable. Do we value poor people less? Our actions perhaps speak loudly of the material status trap that we find ourselves in. Certainly, the lack of self-confidence that many in the West possess demonstrates that for many we lack value in ourselves. For those who have faced redundancy or unemployment, the dramatic collapse of household income can have a devastating and immediate effect. The complexity of property ownership and the suddenness of a loss of income means that immediately downsizing your life in line with your new household budget is not always possible. Especially when considered in the context that job losses tend to occur in a downturn, when jobs are harder to come by and houses are more difficult to sell, and being able to sell at a price that doesn't leave the homeowner in a situation of negative equity is harder.

In the current UK housing market, house prices continue to spiral upward. The housing shortage, especially in the provision of smaller properties and the tightening of the mortgage market, means that affordability has become a real issue. First-time buyers are unable to get on the property ladder because of the need to have a sizeable deposit, and existing mortgage owners are seeing their mortgage costs increase when they re-mortgage, or when their mortgage deal ends, because the interest rates that banks are charging for mortgages are steadily increasing despite the Bank of England rate remaining at 0.5 percent since March 2009. For those struggling to pay their mortgage, the cost of selling a property you own, plus the impact the loss of income has on your ability to borrow, means downsizing becomes an exercise that the poor cannot afford. Property ownership, in an unemployment situation, becomes a trap that is difficult to escape. In the UK you can claim housing benefit to pay rent, but you can't if you own your own home and need support paying your mortgage. The only protection you have is if you have bought payment protection insurance (PPI), but with the PPI scandal in the UK, most of the insurance taken out is not worth the paper it is written on.

The employment market is more uncertain than ever; the abandonment of the Keynesian policy of full employment at the beginning of the 1980s has meant that the capitalist system expects there to be unemployed in society while at the same time berating individuals who find themselves in that situation as lazy or feckless, treating them as a lower class of human being. The unemployed and those on low income become trapped in a cycle of debt, chained to a property they can no longer afford, but can't afford to lose. For the wealthy, property ownership is an expression of the largesse of their wealth, the property portfolio a display of their success. For the majority of homeowners, though, property is their home, a roof over their head and a supposed place of security. A loss of income and unemployment is more than a threat to their wealth; it can spell disaster for a family and have severe consequence on an individual's wellbeing. Our reliance on property ownership and the use of material goods as an expression of security and safety belies the simplicity that capitalism places upon material and consumer goods as status symbols.

Owning property, material goods, and resources isn't anti-Temperatist, but for those with property and resources comes social responsibility. The shift to an ownership society has meant that large swathes of the poor now have a personal debt burden that prevents them from living well and enjoying basic goods and they are just about managing to keep a roof over the head and food on the table. The continuing upward pressure on house prices has meant that the affordability of housing in the UK and in many cities across the globe is beyond the reach of most first-time buyers and adds a significant financial burden to those who are in danger of defaulting on their mortgage or rent, as well as leading to higher living costs. We cannot live in a society where property ownership is increased, while at the same time increasing the debt burden of large sections of the poorest in society and contributing negatively to the plight of those who are homeless.

It is probably fair to say that central planning isn't the answer either. Temperatism isn't another word for socialism. Social housing is a good thing, but the waste that occurs in government social housing planning is no better for the achievement of a program of doing good for society than allowing property ownership to be a source of inequality and instability. The most qualified people to plan and develop social housing are those who plan and develop housing in the commercial market place. Why? The focus and the skill of the private sector is efficiency, doing things right. The focus of the public sector is doing the right things. Combine the two placing the onus on the private sector to pursue doing good, then societal effectiveness can be achieved efficiently. The UK government has gone some way toward addressing the property gap by insisting that planning permission is coupled with the private sector construction plans being inclusive of public buildings such as schools and health centers and also "affordable" housing. But more should be done. One social problem caused by social housing is that it has created ghettos of unemployed and trouble-ridden estates that have become no-go zones even for the police and the geographical separation of the wealthy from the poor. Malcolm Gladwell, in his book *The Tipping Point*, examines New York City in the 1990s, and the steep drop in the citywide crime rate after the introduction of zero tolerance by the New York authorities, including efforts to combat minor crimes occurring on the subway. As Gladwell says, "Epidemics are sensitive to the conditions and circumstances of the times and places in which they occur" (Gladwell, 2000). Currently, the pursuit of profit drives human behavior in the market place. Changing the context from that of capitalism's self-interest to Temperatism's doing good sensitizes the market to doing good and strongly influences the environment that we inhabit, enabling humanity to reassert its social power.

Something has got to change. Once again self-interest has to be replaced with social interest; making profit replaced with doing good. Schemes that think outside the normal paradigms are needed. For example, what if those who were struggling with homelessness were given the support not only to have somewhere to live, but to build their employability at the same time? Impossible? Once again, the challenge is to be inventive and innovative, to focus on doing good. What if those who are suffering from homelessness became involved as apprentices for organizations who have new building projects? It might be that construction companies who are building housing projects take on apprentice plumbers, electricians, plasterers, roofers, joiners, administration assistants, project managers, HR assistants, etc. What if besides getting somewhere to live, the homeless are supported with counseling and financial support systems and the ability to train or learn new skills that will not only help them put a roof over their heads, but give them a future too? Many capitalists will be thinking about the "costs" of such a project without appreciating the holistic approach that saves costs in the long run. For the individuals involved they may well be involved in building the very homes that they end up living in.

There will, of course, be those people who are unable to work, due to ill health, but again housing schemes can be developed alongside appropriate health and wellbeing support. Unemployment must not be equated with fecklessness or individuals being too lazy to work. Unemployment must be seen within the context of the whole society, rather than a problem that should be left for the individual to deal with. We cannot allow people to passively remain within the benefit system, without providing support to help them be all they are meant to be. Many job creation schemes have been attempted in the past, with limited success, partly because the system has relied on the public sector to devise it, a sector that is not used to job creation or wealth creation. A system that is designed from the basis of budgetary constraints will always struggle to add value and provide the necessary tools and parameters to ensure employment for those who have none and will struggle to be efficient. Private organizations offer the necessary foundation, upon which a commitment to ensuring that there is work for all, as far as possible, can be established as a goal for society. The unemployment support system should have a dual role of being a safety net for those who need it and providing the mechanism for proactive support of individuals in developing their talents, using their skills and employing their knowledge. The public sector can provide a layer of support in regard to giving the unemployed public works to do, for higher levels of benefit, alongside training and development opportunities. The aim should always be that someone who is unemployed becomes more able to actively manage their careers and increase their employability as a result of being out of work rather than less so.

Many may criticize ideas such as these as "unrealistic" or "idealistic," but the retort to the cynics has to be the challenge of "why not?" We must as a society begin to think big and realize that we, the human race, are capable of a lot more than we are being given credit for or achieving right now. Capitalism has robbed us not only of our morality, but also of the potential of social power to find a way to make things happen for something other than profit. Power has retreated from the coming together of many in a social movement focused on doing good, which has the ability to unlock the potential of many, to a monetized version of power based on the value that the market places on capital and labor. The market process and capital property disempower the social and political power realms by placing a technical value upon them that represents their worth in an exchange process. As markets have shifted toward financialization, the value of all that is good in society and politics, in that which is meaningful, has diminished in favor of money, profit from capital and capitalist property. The longer we leave the system unchallenged, the harder it will be to uncouple innovation and the ability to make good things happen from monetization and profit agendas.

CHAPTER 8

Attempting to Achieve Economic Democracy

The most highly education generation in the history of the human race, and the best connected, will not accept a future of high inequality and stagnant growth.

—Paul Mason

Democracy in the political sense does strive to reduce inequality. Fundamentally democracy has long been egalitarian; American history particularly has intuitively been linked to the ideal that all men are created equal and in liberal terms. The West purports to pursue the idea of the law of the majority where decisions are made to benefit good to the greatest number, even if the result is a hierarchy of opportunity and wealth. In theory, at least, the mixed market democracy seeks to distribute the wealth created through industrialized modernity equally, eventually. This is in direct contrast to the prevailing economic climate where inequality is accepted as part of the capitalist system and the wealthy elite is more equal than the poor majority. Capitalism's claim that it is democratic is in direct contrast to the reality that the financial and political elite are, through their failure to redistribute wealth fairly, preventing democracy from thriving, even in the so-called liberal democracies of the West. What has become clear from research and empirical evidence is that the larger the public sector is within a market economy, the greater is the level of equality within a democratic society. Far from soft regulation extending democracy, the deregulation and privatization of public utilities from the 1980s has led to the diminishment of democracy understood by conventional wisdom. Studies researching the impact of communist or autocratic states transitioning to democracy, such as Eastern Europe in the early 1990s and more recently Egypt since the Arab Spring, have demonstrated that "there is strong evidence of rising inequality in the democratic transition" (Galbraith, 2012). However, what fast capitalism has contributed to most is that rather than political democracy leading to economic democracy, the outcome is aligned to higher levels of inequality. The associated aspirations of social democracy that should occur following a period of stabilization are never achieved under the capitalism system.

Rather than capitalism contributing to the decline in inequality, it has had the opposite effect, leading to a greater degree of inequality than almost 100 years ago. The gap between the Fortune 500 and FTSE 100 CEOs' salaries and that of their workforce continues to grow, which is even more staggering when you consider the context of the ratio of employees to the 600 CEOs. The market economy does not create an equal platform for all to take the opportunity to prosper; instead it introduces regimented levels of class and status, distributing not only wealth but also power to those who are in a position to succeed under the capitalist structure. Capitalism doesn't believe that each individual is of equal worth, but excuses inequality as inevitable, as if all those who suffer poverty and depravation were always meant to be that way, that if they would just apply themselves with rigor, they would benefit from the system. But reward for hard work doesn't account for the hurdles that those who are born into poverty have to overcome, or the lack of opportunity available to those who have neither the financial resources nor the power connections to make the most of their talent and potential.

Capitalism also assumes that if someone is struggling with their circumstances, it is as a result of their own conduct rather than a result of misfortune or circumstance over which they had no control, not least being an accident of their birth. This not only is unfair, but also does not recognize that our success is based on the proportionality of the opportunities we have had from birth and a large degree of luck. To assume that those who are poor lack motivation, do not work, or enjoy unemployment is to assume the worst of the human condition and lack empathy in regard to the hurt and powerlessness that many have over their own situations. We are not all born equals, and capitalism protects and promotes the continuation of the inequality into which we are born. Just as an economic system should reward for effort, so too should it protect those who are downtrodden due to circumstances. Temperatism argues for providing the poor with a voice, to extend participation beyond what we are born into, increasing the opportunity for control of our destiny and making us more accountable for the privileges our place in society affords us.

The claim that capitalism brings satisfaction is also troubling, since it appears that capitalists will take the credit for the good in society, but it is the government and society's fault that there is poverty and want. This failure to appreciate that capitalism is part of a wider system and is a party in the holistic framework means that economists and the market will claim credit for the good and blame others for its failures. The freedom to choose and to live how you wish, without reference to the wider society and the impact you have upon it, is not the same as democracy. "Democracy affords these processes and values, which is why we must cherish it to the last. Fair democracy—coupled with genuinely competitive, plural markets and the institutions that surround them, which guarantee debates, argument and deliberations—offers the best means to ensure that society is governed by due desert" (Hutton, 2011). Today, the capitalist market owns the mechanisms by which debate and argument can be had. The powerful elite who has an interest in maintaining the status quo orchestrates vitriol for dissenting voices. Protestors are marked out as troublemakers, and critics are slammed for "not understanding" or being "dreamers." The utilitarian economist will defend the capitalist ideal, dismissing new ideas, such as Temperatism, as pathetic, utopian, or not grounded in the real world.

Blaming Regulation for Misdeeds

Those with a capitalist agenda would argue that we cannot replace capitalism and that the question is how much or how little regulation should be in place. For Meltzer, he believes that the call for more regulation is misguided because it

> disregards the fact that a major cause of the [2008 banking] crisis was the failure of national and international regulation. The Basel agreement required banks everywhere to adopt common standards

including a rule that required banks to increase their reserves as they increased their risk position. It never happened. Banks only shifted risk off their balance sheets so as to keep their capital levels low . . . the risk just became less transparent. (Meltzer, 2012)

This circulatory argument is infuriating as well as damning. The purpose of the argument is that financial institutions having too much risk didn't cause the banking crisis and suggests that in creating regulation the regulatory bodies ended up making the banks with too much risk hide the fact that they had too much risk. The lack of responsibility to anything other than self-interest isn't something that can be moderated or smoothed over; it is something that must be changed, and the economic activities of humanity must be recontextualized in regard to its place in a system where social, political, and economic activities impact on each other. This isn't something that can be resolved on a voluntary basis, although there are plenty of organizations that are already stepping up to the plate in regard to offering a sustainability agenda that is along the lines of the Temperatist agenda. Regulation will be needed to begin with to bring corporate capitalism to heel and to begin the task of doing good. Some will come willingly, but many will need to be forced.

The capitalist will often argue that regulation is unnecessary, that the interference of regulation written by lawyers and bureaucrats fails to account for the dynamism of the market place, that the introduction of a piece of regulation at a point in time will result in failure as the market moves on and by default the market will find methods to circumvent the regulation eventually. "Regulation then often misleads the innocent" (Meltzer, 2012). Its true that as new markets emerge, regulation is often behind the curve in regard to managing market forces. Nowhere is this more obvious than with respect to the Internet and social media, which remain largely unregulated or outside of existing regulation because of the fast pace of change. However, the static regulation and dynamic market argument is infuriating and in another context untenable. Taking the argument forward into a different legal context, it therefore follows that we shouldn't try to regulate to stop pedophiles from preying on young people because pedophiles will always find new and inventive ways to abuse young people, and because the way in which pedophiles operate is constantly shifting, we shouldn't draw a line in the sand to say what is or is not acceptable in regard to the sexual exploitations and abuse of children.

This is an extreme example to illustrate a point. To say that we shouldn't regulate the market because the market will always find a way to stop doing good suggests that as a society we should become amoral, as capitalism is. Rather than trying to fight for society to become the very best of everything that humanity has to offer in regard to goodness, we should give up and succumb to the lowest common denominator. The 2012 doping in cycling scandal regarding Lance Armstrong demonstrates what happens when morality is left outside of the equation. Cycling was beset with problems regarding illegal drug taking, with coaches and competitors finding more and more ingenious ways to circumvent the drug tests that cyclists were submitted to. It appears from the reports that have been published that Armstrong became a master at circumventing the drug tests, having never been caught. But cycling has demanded higher standards of itself. Rather than accepting that because everyone is doing it, there is no point trying to stop drug taking, the sport has been at great pains to clean up, and cyclists are now applauded for being clean. Winning is no longer the primary aim of a cyclist, rather it has become about winning fairly.

Profiting from Doing Good

Temperatism seeks the same combination of winning and fairness. The idea behind the new way to think about business does not say that profit is wrong, but it does pursue the best that human society has to offer. It seeks to develop an economic system where profit is a result of doing good, rather than being the only objective outcome of our endeavors, and we hold ourselves to a higher standard in regard to the way we treat the society and world in which we do business, expecting the best, rather than the worst to dominate. Many will argue that a social agenda will fail, because it has failed before. But success needs failure in order to be successful, to learn to be better, to adjust and innovate, and to get it right next time. The reason why change is needed now, more than at any other time in history, is that in 2008 capitalism, most notably the financial markets, circumvented failure and is no longer learning, adapting, or changing its ways in response to getting it wrong. As a system, capitalism believes it is invincible and that it is right—there is no room for change or for criticism to curtail its excesses. To believe that it is possible to divine a system such as capitalism to be more caring or to have a heart is to believe that capitalism has a heart in the first place. Point to any good works at any point in history and you will find behind it, not the capitalist market, but a human who feels that something needs to be done differently. In a mixed market system, the good works, in regard to affordable health, education, and social care, are supported and maintained by the public sector. If you thought that the muscular capitalism of the last 30 years was bad, what will be the result of egotistical capitalism that believes it has a God-like mandate to do as it pleases?

Temperatism doesn't dispute the Kantist view that the human race is imperfect, but it does promote the fact that despite everything, despite our differences and our individual choices, culture, and histories, humanity has the ability to succeed in doing good. We do have a capacity to do evil, but we have a greater capacity for doing good, given the opportunity. Choose your tragedy, man-made or natural. The Second World War, 9/11, Indonesia 2006, Japan 2010, Syria 2012, Nepal 2014, even in the midst of the very worst excesses of mankind, what rises to the surface is a social cohesiveness of protecting the weak, helping the injured, feeding the hungry, roofing the homeless, and shielding the scared. Humanity isn't just about a population of individuals sharing planetary space, it is about a shared purpose and concern for our fellow man. We are more caring, more considerate of others, and greater at doing good than self-interested capitalists would have us believe; it is just that we have forgotten how marvelous we are after decades of having spun lies about being worth it in a self-interested sense.

The Invisible Hand Is a Social Construct

The biggest battleground for the possible rise of Temperatism is that of the market. In researching capitalism, the market is often held up as being the *invisible hand* that is something that has a life and structure of its own, an entity that exists separate from the control and machinations of man. But the fact is that the market is nothing more than a social construct, "fraught with power relations. What 'the market wants' tends to mean what corporations and their bosses want" (Monboit, 2016). The way it operates, the way it reacts to regulation is because of the processes and players that interact and set the rules of the market itself. The market does not exist in a temporal way; it is simply a process by which we choose to interact, existing only as a spiritual realm in which human relatedness occurs. Even the stock market is a figment of our imagination, a list of numbers to which we attribute meaning, but the numbers in and of themselves mean nothing, their physical reality created by machines, displayed digitally or printed onto paper.

If the market does not exist separate from those who create the market, like an organization does not exist separate from the individuals who make up the organization, then it is people that have the power to change the way in which the market operates. The capitalist market is capitalist only because we choose to make it that way through a process of social constructionism. Like anything that is constructed, created, or man-made, it can appear that there is a permanency about it. But like all things man-made, it is possible to unmake them and time can diminish man-made structure in a period of years. The misquoted myth of IBM's Thomas Watson predicting in 1958 that "there would one day be a market for five computers" demonstrates the flimsy nature of human society. We reinvent and remake ourselves all the time. The problem is that capitalism has become a sacred cow that we are afraid to sacrifice.

The housing market is a clear example of a social construct. A house is worth only what the market will pay for it or rather what someone else thinks it is worth. When people stop thinking a house is worth the price tag, it stops being worth that much, and that is when housing booms turn to a housing market slump. When moving to the town I live in, North Wales, in 1997 a three-bedroom Victorian terrace could be bought for £12,000. Can you believe a house was worth so little? Despite the credit crunch, those same houses are valued at over £140,000 (Zoopla, 2017) in a town where the average wage is still around the same level it was in 1997; according to PayScale the average wage in Wrexham is £22,565 (PayScale, 2017). In 1997 you could buy the house with a half a year's salary; fast forward to today, and the same house will cost five times the average salary. In London property prices are higher, with an average terraced house selling for £640,271 (Rightmove, 2017), and the average house price in the UK is £217,502 (Land Registry, 2017). Houses haven't got bigger, the quality of living space is the same as it was when the house was built, but for the average family it now requires two wages to afford to live in that space. As social constructs go, our homes have never been more valuable, and their affordability never more out of reach from the average family.

In our world order at the moment, teachers, nurses, and the police are paid less than footballers, celebrities, and CEOs because we, the people in Western society, have constructed a world where we place more monetary value on one than the other. It's not even that these people produce something of value other than a momentary level of enjoyment and entertainment. Entertainment is an important part of our makeup as human beings, but few would argue that a night at the theater was *more* important than education, or health, or security. It isn't even as if this was always the case. In Victorian times, being in a profession was highly regarded and well rewarded. Even for those born into an aristocratic family, being given a parish was considered an excellent career for a third or fourth son. Florence Nightingale, the founder of modern nursing, came from the Upper Middle class and taking a position as a governess was an acceptable position for middle-class unmarried women. The level of training and education required for those who pursue these careers today is more demanding than ever before, and yet the profession has been devalued. The capitalist marketplace has placed a price on celebrity, and even though players' wages are crippling, the very football clubs they play for, the market justifies their wages. It doesn't have to be this way; if leading football clubs make a decision that they are no longer going to pay players hundreds of thousands of pounds per week, the market will readjust, just as the housing market or stock market readjusts based on perceived value. This phenomenon is beginning to appear in shareholder meetings regarding executive pay, and pay rewards are being recalibrated.

Therefore, if we place value on doing good, then under a Temperatist system those individuals who pursue a career in a role that centralizes in doing good will be more highly valued, and that is a change that would most likely be applauded by the majority. What is more, Temperatism would ensure that each individual is given the opportunity to find out who they are and what value their own personal talent potential is worth by providing a new measure of success beyond pure monetization. Our value as a human being becomes embedded because we are human, not because we can turn a quick profit, earn mega bucks, or afford the latest consumer must have.

Making Good Choices

We are encouraged by capitalism to focus on the fact that we are all different and have differing wants and tastes. What is more, those differences are exploited to separate society into different cliques, fashions, and classes. Take the simple act of buying bread from the supermarket. It is no longer a simple choice between white or brown bread, but what bread you choose to eat separates you into a particular demographic and class. The very range of bread is frankly absurd when you take a step back from being a consumer and matters of personal taste, and notice that today several supermarket aisles are dedicated to bread products. It begs the question, is that really what wealth is for? Capitalism promotes itself as an ideology of freedom and democracy because of its focus on a market that responds to choice. But liberal democracy promotes choice insofar as it does not do harm to others. There is so much choice in our society that we now have the tyranny of choice. As the number of options from which we can choose multiplies, so does the effort required to make the choice. At some point, too much choice makes it difficult to be able to distinguish the best choice and therefore the consumer no longer benefits from the extra choice to which they are subjected. In the wealthy West, we have access to so much choice and more information than it would be possible to consume in a lifetime that it is becoming impossible to know whether the choices we make are good choices or bad choices. But capitalism is self-interested when it comes to offering more choice. In order to drive profit, growth is needed and growth needs additional consumption. Consumers will consume more only when there are more options about what we can consume. No longer content with brown leather boots, we are bombarded with shoes for every occasion and every outfit. Any parent will know that in order to bring up children to understand good and bad there has to be limits to the choice and an encouragement to make good choices whether that is with food, behavior, bedtimes, activities, or school. But as a parent, the choices that our children want, in regard to their favorite foods, bedroom furniture, toys, clothes, and activities, extend far beyond the realms of good and bad and blurs the lines between needs and wants.

Society sets the boundary for what good is in any given context. In the UK, society deems that it is good for children to attend school, turn up on time, respect the teachers, and make an effort to learn. Parents in the UK are held to account, and if their children don't attend school and they make no effort to respond to truancy, then parents can and have been fined or even sent to prison. School reports are sent outlining academic achievement and parents are encouraged to partner with the school to help their child's educational development. Children don't have a choice in the UK about whether they will or will not receive education until they are 16 and there are moves to increase the age to 18. Many children in countries around the world don't have the freedom to receive an education, either because of politics, religion, war, or poverty. But in the UK education is not a choice, but is given free as part of our democratic right. Our freedom makes it compulsory to attend free education until the age of 16. It appears, therefore, that unlimited choice is not always good and freedom sometimes means that our choices are made for us. Capitalists would argue that it is paternalistic to set parameters for common good such as education, health, or infrastructure, including roads, sewerage, and water supply. But it is subjective as to what point doing good stops being good and begins to interfere with our freedom. According to capitalism, any regulation, intervention, or interference is theoretically a bad thing purely because it is interfering with the purity of the market. But with an agenda that is focused on profit as a primary goal, is it any wonder that we have ended up in a position where what we are being told is good for us is actually doing more harm than good, is leaving a large section of society poor and a select few wealthy, and is reducing responsibility to the lowest common denominator rather than empowering individuals with an expectation that they have a responsibility to something bigger than mere individual self-interest.

Capitalism and neoliberal theory promote a dichotomy and conflict between private and public, state and market, when in fact there is a mutual interdependency between the economic, political, and social elements of our society, which means that they maintain and support each other. Temperatism with its focus on changing the market agenda to deliver a primacy of doing good and profit for purpose isn't looking to destroy the opportunity or mechanism to create wealth. Rather it seeks to address the current disfigurement of market practices that has led to villainy and social welfare reductionism, which will ultimately result in the destruction of society and nature. If it is possible to assume that growing levels of inequality in society can be described as freedom, then, for the majority, an intervention that changes the focus of the market and readdresses the distribution of power between the social, political, and economic realms is no less free, especially as the market is a social construction and as such should be constructed for the benefit, empowerment, and betterment of the majority.

The Numbers to Change the System

Is such as transformation possible? Genghis Khan transformed self-seeking, disparate Mongol tribes into a strong nation in a generation. Churchill constructed a system that enabled a poor and weak country to pull together to stand up to fascist tyranny. Wilberforce pulled together the most unlikely of allies to succeed in pushing through a parliamentary act for the abolition of slavery, despite the majority of parliamentarians being slave owning. All things are possible if there is a heart and mindfulness to make it so. Temperatism has both. Capitalism has neither.

Human society is made up of political, economic, and social elements; they cannot be separated and each part is part of a wider system of cause and effect. Currently we can look at the government, society, and economy and come to the conclusion that the market is in control. Since the government has the responsibility to regulate the market and protect society, we begin to understand the size of the problem we are faced with. Those who support the free market would argue that regulation or intervention is problematic. Democracy is about power. Capitalism marginalizes power to those who have the economic resources to defend it, at the expense of the wider society. People power is what will be needed to disperse power across society and across political, economic, and social boundaries. This is more than taxpayers and voters demanding fairness and holding organizations to account for the external costs of their operation, but rather a redefinition of the role of organizations, the purpose of the market, and the demand for a different agenda.

If government regulation and legal restraints are not the answer, then what is? The truth is that the answer lies in the very organizations that currently pursue the capitalist profit agenda, as well as in every individual within society. There are more employees than employers and there are more consumers than suppliers. For those of us that inhabit management positions, we can make decisions that are based on doing good, before making profit. CEOs and shareholders can choose to invest an organization's time and resources into a wider context in regard to return on investment. Consumers can choose to buy products and place their money in the hands of credit unions rather than big business and banks. To say that you don't have time to do these things is to accept the way things are. If you are unhappy with the way society is, then change really does begin with the man in the mirror. In democracy citizens have to take part in democratic processes to ensure that power is kept in check. Perhaps the most encouraging outcome of the Trump presidency is a realization by the apathetic that their voice and vote count. Not just in America, but around the world, citizens are finding their voice again, and they are taking action to be heard.

Currently, power is one sided—organizations have the money to fight, both in terms of marketing and in regard to lawsuits to keep at bay consumers—but the social media is out of their hands, very often bypassing the gagging orders and restrictions of an autocratic government to highlight the true voice of the people. Consumers and citizens are discovering how powerful this mechanism can be in the West. The biggest weapon that capitalism has right now is indifference or the belief that our voice won't make a difference. But the underprivileged exist in both rich and poor nations; the numbers who have seen a demise in their quality of life far outstrip those who have seen wealth flow into their personal reserves. There is a germinating realization that all of us deserve and can create a society where equality is possible. Temperatism doesn't pursue a world of *flat-earth egalitarians* but neither does it believe that the financial world should benefit at the expense of those that create the value. Profit must be considered in proportion to the value creators. The continuing gap between the haves and their lack of contribution to wider society and the have nots who create value is an injustice that society cannot continue to stand back and allow.

A current example in the continuing practice of UK is energy suppliers increasing the prices of gas and electricity just as winter starts. Many people, not just the old and infirm, live in fuel poverty, where more than 10 percent of their income goes on heating and lighting their homes. As November rolls around, news reports are full of people frightened of turning on their heating because they will be unable to pay their bills, this at a time when the energy companies are reporting hundreds of millions of pounds in profit. In the 1980s the British government opened the energy market to competition, removing the state monopoly and privatizing the energy companies at the time. The idea was to introduce competition into the marketplace and improve service to the public. Services haven't improved and the *big six* large players who all seem to increase their prices at the same time dominate competition. At the same time the UK is entering a period in history where energy supply is going to become problematic. It is reported that the UK will soon begin to experience regular power outages and energy shortages. In a capitalist marketplace scarce resources also equate to an increase in prices. This isn't about luxury goods, but about households being able to keep warm and light their homes. It is true that energy consumption has increased per capita as the number of appliances we rely on in modern life have increased, but for many of the most vulnerable in society and those greatly affected by the energy price rises, they don't have several televisions, computers, or mobile phones. They seek simply to heat their home, cook, refrigerate their food, and turn the light on when it gets dark. The current solution is that energy companies are offering to insulate homes in the UK for a discounted rate, or in some cases at no cost to help make homes more energy efficient.

But more could be done. A Temperatist approach would suggest that the energy companies take the poorest in society and help make them net producers of energy. The installation of solar panels on the homes of those suffering from fuel poverty might seem like madness to those with a profit-first approach. But if the ideological approach were focused on doing good, then it would make sense.

First, it means that those who once couldn't afford to pay for their basic energy needs, who are suffering from fuel poverty, can once again heat and light their homes without fear of a bill they can't afford. In fact, not only does energy stop being a cost to the poorest in society, but rather offers the opportunity of becoming an income generator, although at a lower level than if the household had installed the system privately. Secondly, the energy companies benefit because they take those who can't afford to buy their energy out of the net consumption equation into a net positive generator of electricity, providing a steady supply of excess energy to the national grid at relatively low cost and low maintenance to the energy companies. All this while contributing to the increasing percentage of clean energy supplies and reducing the carbon footprint in the UK.

The wider UK population will also benefit because the cost and efficiency of solar panels and the energy collection infrastructure and technology will improve because the energy companies will want to deliver the program in the most efficient way possible, which will drive innovation in regard to materials, cost, and generation capacity. This in turn will promote affordable solar energy among private householders producing a further reduction in residential energy consumption, ensuring that vital energy supplies can be used for industry as energy shortages begin to bite and help the UK navigate, or possibly avoid, a period of possible social unrest because of power shortages.

Many will read the above and declare that this is too simplistic, that it is not as easy as all that. But no one is promising doing good will be easy. For a start the cultural shift required to make such new thinking the norm is far harder than flicking a light switch to the on position. But this is the great thing about the human race. We are inventive, and anything *is* possible. Give us a problem and we *will* find a solution; it might be difficult, it might seem impossible, but we can rise to the challenge, and in doing so advance our society. If it is possible for a man to free-fall from the edge of space, why do we doubt our capacity to invent, innovate, and develop the means to improve our society for the benefit of everyone? The fact is that whenever industry has been challenged to do things differently, to change the way that they go about their business by regulation or societal demands, they have. They might have moaned about it. They might have declared that the end was nigh by being made to do things a certain way, but it never was. There will be many who will struggle with the transformation. There will be a great number who will fight against it, block it, and barricade the way we do things around here but, if and only if, a few good men and women, indomitable in spirit and with great tenacity, decide that we can and can influence those who will, then all things are possible.

If you are a leader of an organization, then the challenge is to consider how your organization could do things differently, to contribute to doing good. Begin with the end point of doing good as an outcome, and adopt new thinking about the way your organization goes about its business.

CHAPTER 9

Good Citizenship Is Good Business

Citizenship is establishing itself as the requisite mind-set for doing business in the 21st Century

—Ged Hedstrom

Over the past few years there has been an increasing recognition by organizations that there is a need to accept that they are responsible to a growing body of core stakeholders, suppliers, customers, employees, society, and government. With the growth in stakeholder management, organizations have at last begun to realize that good citizenship is good for business. Furthermore, there is evidence that there are green shoots of understanding, that there is a moral choice to be made in regard to wealth distribution. Social harmony is believed to be the proper choice by many, but not all organizations or individuals would voluntarily give up their own self-interest or profit agenda to achieve it. Many capitalists would argue that changing responsibility from that of return on investment to its shareholders to that of a wider stakeholder model is little more than an attack on free market principles and is an indication of irresponsible management of the organization's resources. Good citizenship, therefore, is to capitalism little more than a violation of the principle that bigger profits lead to better standards of living and that by not trying to achieve the highest profits possible, or by offering, for example, employees a better benefits package than the market can bear is reckless. However, what is becoming apparent through research is that wealth redistribution isn't simply a one-sided bargain, whereby those who have given away what they have for the sole benefit of the recipient. What organizations and philanthropic individuals are discovering is that doing good has a net benefit, which returns favorable outcomes to the giver as well as the receiver. Decisions about wealth redistribution, therefore, exceed simple mathematics regarding rich to poor, inequality to fairness, profit to corporate social responsibility but instead offer a mutually beneficial outcome that all can sign up to. Results show that it is possible to invest in doing good and yet benefit from sustainable healthy profits at the same time. Thus, it is possible that delivering social harmony provides more stable market conditions and less dramatic levels of boom and bust.

Temperatism goes beyond the triple bottom line of people, planet, and profit, which is advocated by sustainable business consultants and the approach currently taken by organizations with an interest in sustainability. The multiple shareholder approach is progress, but can still be viewed in the context of a furthering of self-interest that is at the heart of the capitalist system. Marx used the term *appropriation* to describe the character of organizations in pursuing profit-first motives, noting "that capitalists appropriate, or commandeer, the surplus produced by labor and do not remunerate them for it" (Stokes, 2011).

Organizations still only implement policies based on the business case, rather than because it is the right thing to do. Meyer (2015) offers the concept of "doing well," which is defined as "marked improvements in terms of multilevel performance including economic, human, and environmental aspects, indicating the magnitude of change in an upward trajectory, and highlighting future viability and sustainability." The argument is that there is a corresponding relationship between "doing good" and "doing well," in that organizations which do good perform better economically delivering outstanding financial results. However, "'doing good' is not considered a means towards 'doing well' (profit/economic performance). Profitability or economic improvements are an effect of 'doing good' . . . 'Doing good' is an authentic, unselfish way to shape beneficial situations for everyone" (Meyer, 2015).

Today, the majority of organizational commitment to good corporate citizenship is as a result of key factors such as pressure groups, fear of regulation from government, issues with attracting and retaining talent, and increased competitive advantage requiring the organization to make themselves more attractive to investors and customers who have a different agenda than a black-and-white return on investment. But what started as something that could be viewed as a cynical attempt by capitalist organizations to avoid interference in the market has extended to a genuine rise in organizations and government bodies attempting to do good and seeing the positive effects of doing good on their bottom line.

At the forefront of the current *good citizenship* model is the green business movement. Since government regulation on climate change issues is inevitable, many organizations are preparing themselves ahead of time by changing their business model and integrating green business practices into their day-to-day business operations. Even the presidential executive orders to remove climate change regulation in the United States will not completely reverse the progress made, because businesses have seen the economic benefits of environmental protectionism. Therefore, it is not just the threat of government regulation that is changing organizational behavior, rather the discovery that good citizenship is good business. For example, "FedEx's new fuel efficient hybrid trucks reduce fuel expenses by more than a third while shrinking smog-causing emissions by two-thirds and nearly eliminating particular emissions, the company reports" (CQ Researcher, 2010). The result is more than good PR. As well as appealing to customers who may be willing to pay more for friendly products such as responsibly sourced fish, sustainable products, or organic foods, employee turnover reduces, cost savings and efficiencies are found, and innovation and creativity increase. It could be argued that organizational performance improves because an organization is purposeful and intent on doing good. The CIPD conducted a survey in December 2010 called *Shared Purpose: The Golden Thread*. It showed that organizations that have a purpose achieve better results in both financial measures such as profitability and people measures, including improved employee engagement and productivity. Research studies conducted by Gallup have showed that engaged employees are 18 percent more productive, 12 percent more profitable, 60 percent less likely to leave the organization, and take less time off sick—2.7 days per year versus 6.3 days for disengaged staff. Good citizenship therefore provides more than a good feeling. Doing good creates a healthy exchange of benefit for both society and the organization.

The societal benefits of higher incomes, better health, education, training, and employability are matched by corporate benefits such as higher work motivation, higher productivity, and lower absenteeism. Investments up to the point where none of the participating subjects (or institutions) can be made better off without another subject being made worse off (in absolute terms) are therefore good management practices. (Leisinger, 2007)

Many organizations are now working alongside pressure groups, such as the Carbon Trust, to develop and adopt a robust corporate social responsibility (CSR) policy and program. As well as reducing the impact on the external costs of operations on the wider environment, many organizations are promoting their role in improving the wider society and providing enhanced employee benefits package that goes well beyond the remuneration that the market would dictate for workers in the industry. The growing concerns caused by globalization and the rise in the use of technology have increased the interest in organizations doing things differently, not just for investors and customers, but also for the wider stakeholder community. The transparency created by social media means that the wider global community could now examine every organization in regard to social responsibility. Governments and organizations are more aware than ever of the pressure from ordinary people. This pressure coupled with the advances in social media means any ministerial gaff or corporate misdemeanor can spread across the globe in a matter of seconds, doing untold damage to corporate reputations and resulting in significant consequences to the bottom line. Power has begun to shift away from politicians, government regulators, and organizational leaders, instead reverting to those who use the new information super-highways to promote and market their objections to abhorrent business practices. If ever there was a time in history where fundamental change could happen and happen rapidly, it is now. We are no longer reliant on people being in the right place at the right time, or having access to vast reserves of wealth to push for reform. Having the means to hold the accountable responsible gives individuals the motivation to stand up and be counted. We are now equipped to challenge the system, to reject passivity and prevent the capitalist system from fooling us into believing we can't make a difference.

Temperatism itself is not simply a promotion of corporate social responsibility or the welfare state, although both these ideas contribute to how Temperatism may be achieved in our society. CSR, which Veldsman (2015) defined as "an organisation acting in an ethical, responsible and sustainable manner in its intentions, decisions, actions, and impact towards its context," does not solve the issues of fast capitalism, profit-first agendas, and the deregulated labor market that have led capitalism to have such widespread negative effects on the workers. Equally, socialism did not democratize the ownership of the means of production; rather its history demonstrates it promotes political power and elitism over the power of capital. The fight is not to do what we have always done, but to promote doing good as a new agenda, with new ideas, creativity, and innovation to support it. The fight is to change the focus of what we do, as well as how we do what we do. Instead of allowing organizations to hide behind complex multi-country structures that create a barrier between the corporate machinations and the society in which they operate, there needs to be an increased visibility. We need to develop more transparency of both what organizations are doing and awakening our awareness of how other people are living. This isn't an excuse to gawk at the lives of the super-rich or persecute us with the despair of the amount of suffering in the world, but rather to shine a light on the ugly truth of our current predicament. We must hold a magnifying glass over the levels of individual consumption and the impact that our pursuit of consumerism is having on the wider society and the environment. Sky's Ocean Rescue in the UK is an example of one such magnifying glass that is focusing on the impact of disposable single-use plastic on the ocean environment. The campaign blends the organization's capacity for investigative reporting with a doing good agenda. Organizations are set up to encourage us to consume and compare our consumption to the aspirational advertisements in media and also make comparisons in regard to our peer group. This gives us an unreality about the true wealth that we may have and indeed the house of cards that is holding up the consumption of our neighbors. It was shocking that during the U.S. election 2016, portions of the electorate, and now government, are still in denial about the dangers of climate change. This ignorance of the truth of our situation cannot continue.

Organizations Make Temperatism Possible

Therefore, an essential actor in the Temperatist ideology are organizations and their impact and influence on the socially constructed marketplace. Meltzer complains that "after 25 to 40 years of talk, promises and proposals about energy, education, health care and cocaine and other drugs little if any progress is visible on these issues." (Meltzer, 2012). These issues are as important to corporate life as they are to society. Power cuts and high energy prices impact profit; education affects the ability of organizations to find the skills, knowledge, and talent required for their operations; and the health of the population affects the cost to organizations of absence and sickness of their employees. The Temperatist approach to these problems is not to enlarge the size of the state, but increase the responsibility of organizations in these areas, again with a mandate of doing good. There is no acknowledgment that capitalism is to blame for the lack of progress in these areas, even though the energy market in the United States and UK is dominated by private organizations, and organizations are involved in the education and healthcare sectors. It is not criminal organizations, but organizations pursuing profit, which are involved in the market for illegal substances. Criminal or legal, organizations behave the way they do, in order to gain support from their core stakeholders. It is the systems that we create, through regulation, law, and socially constructed rules that govern the behavior of organizations. To complain about the way organizations act, even if they are acting legally, is directing our efforts in the wrong place. The institution of capitalism begets bad citizenship, which adjusts only when organizations are pressured to adopt different practices, such as CSR. If investors invest only in organizations that act as good citizens, then good citizenship will become good business.

The issues and faults that belie the benign promotion of capitalism have been hidden by the focus of issues and problems being the fault of individual behavior, individual circumstances, and individual failings. If we examine the outcome of the August 2011 riots in the UK, the actions by government were against individual rioters and a focus of resources was on identifying, arresting, and punishing each individual. Although there was some debate at the time as to the reasons for the riots and some examination of the social ills that led to the actions taken, it is hard to tell if any resource was committed to addressing the very problems that led to the riots in the first place. The riots were diminished from being a big social problem to being addressed as a group of individuals who needed to be dealt with separately. We were so busy pointing our fingers at the individuals involved that we forgot to address the bigger questions regarding good citizenship:

- Is it right that our economic system leaves whole sections of society underemployed or unemployed?
- What damage is a lack of investment into the talent potential of the rioters having on the individuals' ability to partake in their role of citizen?
- How can we help these individuals feel empowered in a manner that doesn't require violence?

As we dismissed the rioters as a few bad apples, we stand by as all the while the negative changes we have experienced in society continue to grow, because the problems of individuals added together is a bigger problem than the sum of the individual parts. Therapy and self-help books won't fix the world's problems, but a focus on social citizenship will. It is not enough to say that individuals are responsible for their actions toward society, if we do not hold organizations to the same level of accountability. Good citizenship is more than just doing the right things because they are morally promotable, but rather because there is the recognition that there are greater social and economic benefits associated with strategies, which consider the long-term effects of how businesses operate in the wider environmental context. If society, government, and organizations really wish to achieve the outcomes that good citizenship offers, then the principles upon which organizations are founded need to change fundamentally. Instead of *make profit and individuals will benefit*, the clarion call should be *doing good and being good citizens will make a profit*. Organizations cannot operate separately from society. Not only are their employees part of the society in which the organization operates, but so too are the other stakeholders, the products and services provided, and the external costs of operation that may be unseen, but still impact on society. When organizations do not act as good citizens, there is no reason to expect that their employees, customers, suppliers, or the wider community will either. But how does doing good move beyond simple CSR policies, rather as a reflection of a whole attitude and spirit in which organizations operate in society?

Doing Good Is an Everyday Operation

For Temperatism, doing good is not limited to *how* an organization does its business in regard to mere processes, but *what* it does, the inputs and outcomes, *when* it acts, *who* it is acting on behalf of, and *where* it focuses its efforts. Outcomes are a result of everything that goes into an organization. If everything that goes into the day-to-day operations of the business is corrupted or misaligned with a doing good agenda, then doing good as an outcome is impossible. Today there is evidence that doing good is extending beyond simple policies and day-to-day operations. Andrew Savitz, formerly of PWC said, "A generation of people in search of deeper meaning in their lives is now taking over the corporate suites" (CQ Research, 2010). Boardrooms are being filled with individuals who believe that organizations have a responsibility that is wider than just producing bigger profits for their shareholders. Entrepreneurs are starting businesses that have doing good at the heart of their organizations' mission and values, and which are in turn becoming very successful in the marketplace. A whole industry has developed that offers investors a different measure of organizational success, from funds that focus exclusively on organizations that have a good record of wider responsibility to indexes that are designed to measure the financial performance of organizations with a track record in good CSR. These examples are more than purely an acknowledgment that social responsibility is on an agenda somewhere but recognition that there are investors who believe that social responsibility and doing good matters and should have primacy. Organizations have realized that having a strong reputation for CSR helps them to combat negative PR when things do go wrong. But organizations need to go further than reputation management; they must see themselves "as an inherent part of the intricate fibre and DNA of the communities/societies in which they operate . . . acting as trusted custodian of the assets of the communities/societies in which they are embedded and operating" (Veldsman, 2015). Taking part in doing good allows for mistakes to be made, albeit not too often. The impact on reputation and investor confidence is therefore a critical component of good citizenship being good business. This recognition is essential if we are to consider a market with a different agenda. If Temperatism is to succeed in persuading organizations that they need to change their agenda to doing good, those same organizations must be assured that they can continue operating with access to an investment market, which is necessary for them to finance their operations. If investors did not exist and did not react, negatively or positively, to events pertaining to doing good, then Temperatism would be a nonstarter. But reputation can matter in equal measure to that of competitive advantage, when it comes to those who invest in organizations.

Measuring Doing Good

The difference that a doing good agenda has on the citizenship question is that judgment regarding good management of an organization's resources goes beyond short-term finance reporting, but will be based on a long-term strategic viewpoint of whether the choices that an organization is making contribute to sustainability and doing good. This has implications for the governance of organizations in regard to the role of investors and their involvement in the long-term sustainability of organizational decisions. Investors will quickly establish which organizations are having a positive impact on their stakeholder group and will have confidence in an organization with a strong reputation for doing good, as well as the accompanying financial performance. Demonstrating a lead in social performance "infused with a sense of rightness, publically stated as doing the right (or good) thing for the right reasons, in the right way, at the right time" will become the new measure of good management practices, alongside the delivery of long-term financial performance measures (Veldsman, 2015). Stakeholder value is not an alien measure, as it has long been recognized there is a wider definition of stakeholder beyond the traditional financial investor. But Temperatism offers the foundation, in regard to basic goods, as to whether organizations are delivering as a good citizen with a wider doing good agenda.

However, Temperatism aims for organizations to establish doing good beyond simple CSR policies and reputational management. Instead, Temperatism wants to restructure the primary role of organizations to that of a doing good first and foremost. Good citizenship emphasizes a number of key areas for corporate responsibility from caring employee practices, enhancing the local and where pertinent the global community and wider society in which the organization operates, and positively impacting the environment and delivering shareholder value. Currently, CSR practices are supported as long as they can be shown to be good for business. However, too often the gap between what is good from a short-term profit perspective and what is good for society as whole and sustainable long-term profits is too great a gap for organizations to cross. Duty of care should first and foremost be to the wider society and profit second, if the full possibility and opportunity afforded by good corporate citizenship is to be fully realized. The hesitancy with embracing doing good is the difficulty many organizations have in measuring their success at improving wider stakeholder value, leading to questions as to how to measure whether an organization is or is not doing good. One of the reasons why monetization is so attractive to humanity is that it is easy to measure. A positive number on the bottom line is success, a negative number failure. But when it comes to doing good, finding a measure that would judge whether organizations are achieving a doing good outcome is difficult to measure mathematically or with concrete certainty. There has been much research on whether socially responsible firms deliver better return on investment than those who do not engaged in CSR, so the market already has mechanisms to decide who to include in socially responsible indices and who do not match that criteria.

It would certainly be a challenge for those embracing Temperatism to develop a consensus over what should be measured, how it is measured, and what the rewards should be to support organizations that embrace good citizenship.

Certainly, being able to demonstrate that the organization is contributing to the delivery of improvement in areas of basic goods would be a start point for how doing good might be measured. Suggesting that the economic targets are set for basic goods is easy to write on paper, but this, of course, begins with a need to answer the question of how much is enough in regard to basic goods. How much is enough is being explored by experiments in universal basic income, which are explored in various nations to pay citizens a basic income to unemployed citizens such as in Canada and Switzerland. In Finland "two thousand unemployed people will be given €560 every month for two years, without restrictions or conditions" (Kentish, 2016). The goal of such income experiments is to promote employment by removing incentive traps caused by social welfare payments, reduce inequality, and cut welfare spending. This might seem backward, giving people more to cost less, but giving everyone certainty of income removes the disabling impact of inequality. There would also be debate as to what measures are appropriate to address immediate issues of poverty, climate change, and specific social issues that need to be addressed. Having the end in mind in order to create a set of measures is essential to decide whether actions taken moves the society toward the goal or away from it. Once again there is a faith in humanity's ability to invent and create methods to measure success. These measures already exist in many organizations and bodies who are seeking to extend their understanding of the outcomes of their activities.

The Temperatist model makes one significant swing in regard to economic ideology. Instead of relying on a process of tax and spend for redistributing wealth, it exposes the producers of wealth to their true position in society.

The market becomes the center stage in ensuring that basic goods and societal needs are protected. It becomes the goal of organizations to not just ensure that society flourishes, for the lucky few, but also to encourage the weak and dispossessed to be raised up by the rest of society. Decisions will need to be made on how best to ensure that the most good can be extracted from organizational endeavors. Rather than creating a position where avoiding responsibility and external cost creates winners and losers in the market, organizations will be the architects of a win–win between private and public gains. This is different from a hopeful trickle-down, but rather it is a sharing of success and responsibility; as society flourishes, so too will the organization. The organization will have the skills and knowledge they need for their operations because they will be investing in it, not at a cost to competitive advantage, but in advancing it. Societal problems and issues will no longer be the responsibility of someone else but in everyone's interest to work together and collaborate in resolving. As organizations are already discovering with CSR initiatives, doing good also creates a space for innovation that minimizes waste, improves efficiency, and finds long-term solutions to scarce resources. Doing good offers the opportunity to create a society that is more stable and more equal, something necessary for a healthy market.

The final thought on good citizenship being good business is the current situation of expensive sticking plaster solutions to major problems in our society. Most issues faced by organizations are as a result of systemic problems in our society as a whole. Consider, if you will, the cost to organizations of theft and the cost that organizations have to pay for security measures required to protect the organization against theft, or the cost of absence and the cost of the processes and mechanisms required to manage absence in an organization. These two examples are just two of any number of organizational issues that are increasing and adding a significant cost to organizations, caused primarily by inequality. The cost of the savings organizations make in regard to paying minimum wages, lean workforces, and people costs in general have led, directly and indirectly, to additional costs and resource being committed to solve the unintended consequences of the cost savings made in the first place.

We are not richer for organizations avoiding doing good, but instead are forced to commit more resource and energy than ever before to fix the problems caused by bad citizenship behaviors. It will take time to clear up the mess of our mistakes and bring things back into balance, but the longer we continue to do the wrong thing, the bigger the mess will get. It's not a case of whether organizations should be doing good; it is how long it will take for them to realize that being good citizens is good business.

CHAPTER 10

People and Purpose Before Profit

Insanity: doing the same thing over and over again and expecting different results.

—Albert Einstein

Capitalism as an ideology expresses the idea that the purpose of organizations is to grow and deliver profit for their shareholders. We accept this, almost blindly. Since 2008, a new specter of inequality has begun to be reported in regard to tax avoidance and evasion, with respect to both wealthy individuals and big businesses. The observation is that although the individuals and organizations involved are not doing anything illegal, their actions are morally wrong. When Amazon, Google, and Starbucks were exposed for not paying any corporation tax on UK sales, many would have shrugged their shoulders and asked what all the fuss was about. All organizations set themselves up to be as efficient as possible, and to pay the least amount of tax that they legally get away with, that's just good business sense. These companies aren't doing anything illegal, they are just structuring themselves to avoid paying too much tax so they can make more profit and increase shareholder return.

However, there remains an important question, Why? It might seem like a childish question to ask why is it important that an organization make more profit; after all anyone who has ever been involved in business will understand the financial drivers of a business. But the question is an important one. Why earn more profit and for what reason? Obvious answers are, of course, that an organization needs profit in order to continue trading and it is also important to provide shareholders with a return on their investment in the business, so more investment can be made to keep the investment flowing. Profit from operations can be used to invest in the business to ensure it stays in business, stays competitive, and stays profitable. All sound business reasons for the pursuit of profit. But I return once more to the question of profit for what purpose? Why should an organization want to stay in business? For what reason do organizations exist in our society?

With the financialization of our economic system and societal values, the conclusion I have come to is that the pursuit of profit for the sake of profit has become seemingly circular. The key differentiator between Temperatism and capitalism is that human endeavor and effort and resources used for profit and wealth creation should be for a purpose beyond additional profit and wealth creation. A farmer would not grow crops to create seed so that he can plant more crops and for no other reason. It would be pointless. I believe that the purpose of profit must be for the betterment of humanity. We work hard and use our inventiveness and creativity to come up with new ways of making money because we want things to be better.

The global economic system and the true cost to society of our reliance on the capitalist market have been exposed by the credit crunch. Financial truths have been buried under the rubble of lies told by the numbers. The pursuit of short-term profit and financial success has hidden the costs to the long-term health of both our economy and our society. We now have the facts at our fingertips to challenge financialization and the conventions of capitalism at both a market system and a societal level. The truth is that the capitalist pursuit of self-interest is not compatible with sustainability, either in the environmental sense or in the sense of social good and equality of wealth creation. Self-regulation fails to contain the *greed is good* mentality, and financial results are an inadequate measure of the true impact of the external costs created by the profit agenda. Many organizations have made our lives better with their products and services, but for other organizations they don't produce anything that advances the betterment of humanity. If organizational profit isn't used to contribute to improving the health, education, security, and wellbeing of society as a whole, then we must begin to challenge its purpose.

Profit for Purpose

Profit for purpose might take the form of a contribution to the society in which the organization operates, through corporate social responsibility or paying corporation tax, but also the way in which they treat their employees. It's not that profit is bad and there should be reward for those who take the risk with investment in business. So the return on investment to shareholders isn't the problem. But Temperatism challenges us to consider what the purpose of all our activity is really for. Research shows that as we get more wealth, our happiness actually reduces. If the top one percent in society are getting richer and the rest of us are getting poorer and more miserable, then we cannot passively accept that there is nothing wrong when organizations structure themselves purely for the purposes of making more profit. Sooner rather than later we must pursue the *why* and *for what* purpose question regarding profit. If we don't, then it will be crisis that will cause these questions to be asked. When our water, food, energy, security, healthcare, and education reach the crisis point, it will be too late to say to organizations that they need to take their proper place in society and begin focusing on profit as a vehicle for doing good, because organizations will be in a prime position to make more profit as an end in itself.

It is remarkable that for all our advancements in efficiency and technical achievements, and despite the industrialization of scientific inventiveness, the management of human affairs continues to be focused on the numerical outputs of our endeavors. Even looking back merely a decade, we can see that modern society is phenomenal in its ability to create. Despite this we are unhappier, more depressed, and suffering from higher levels of anxiety than at any other point in history. It seems like the real outcome of progress is misery. Scientific management has provided the means by which we can measure our worth and our value, to plot our status and climb up, or fall from, the social ladder. The higher up the ladder we are, the more successful we believe we are, all the while growing more anxious about losing the status we have achieved. We are left bereft of friendship and community while at the same time driven to consume what we can no longer afford, eating what is no longer healthy, and drinking excessively or taking illegal drugs to dull the pain. We must be able to expect more from the amazing inventiveness of humanity. Otherwise our efforts will only achieve a continuing decline in our own wellbeing and the threat of further breakdown in our society.

Valuing Individuals Equally

The result of our measurement is that we no longer value each human life equally. The military term *collateral damage* has wormed its way into our social and business lexicon to justify the results of our actions that harm other people. Conferring of status helps us all sanitize and justify wasted talent potential and worse still enable us to ignore the wasted lives of those whose talents are left to rot in bowels of forgotten sections of society. I don't believe it is acceptable to refuse to do all we can, everything in our power, to stop the preventable wasting of talent of a single individual. Research demonstrates that our society is more cohesive when rank and status is replaced by equality. The more equal a society is, the more sociable we become, and our true humanity can be released more fully. Equality is more than simple redistribution of wealth; it is the creation of a society "in which we are less ranked, devalued, psychologically shaped and constrained by status, in which our position in the social class hierarchy imprints itself on us less indelibly from early life onwards, in which the purpose of life and the idea of success are less dominated by and reduced to the idea of being better than or superior to our fellow human beings" (Dorling, 2011). As we pursue greater levels of profitability and wealth creation, the evidence suggests that we have gone past the point of gaining any real benefit from the machinery of economic growth, and instead the growing levels of inequality are leading to an increasingly broken society and a broken economy. While growth should provide the vehicle to benefit the poor, instead it is the wealthy that get richer, at the expense of the poor. "Typically, the poorest half of the population get something like 20 or 25 per cent of all incomes and the richest half get the remaining 75 to 80 per cent" (Wilkinson and Pickett, 2010). In addition, we have only just begun to face up to the fact that the environmental impact of our efforts could spell the end of life on earth. It feels like we have pushed the self-destruct button and are powerless to take the actions necessary to turn it off.

Human beings are born with a heart and soul that yearns for more than profit. Evidence shows that purpose that is purely a profit goal does not engage employees, but instead they want to be part of an organization that has a purpose, which resonates with their own personal inner purpose. The reason organizations such as Virgin and Innocent Drinks have such a committed workforce is that both organizations pursue a purpose that switches people on—and the outcome is greater and, more importantly, sustainable profit and wealth for all. Too few organizations realize that a purpose is needed at the heart of their operations in order to be successful and deliver sustainable performance. The more opportunity that individuals have to put effort, hard work and their talent into something that achieves a purpose that they can align to, the more the individual will develop discretionary work habits and devote themselves to the achievement of high levels of performance.

In organizational life, our value to an organization is based on price. How much we are paid, how much we cost the company to employ us, is recorded in minute detail on workforce spreadsheets and on an outgoing line on the profit-and-loss statement. Human beings with all their potential, knowledge, skills, and talent are boiled down to a number.

> Marx's critique of capitalism was fundamentally moral. It was, he thought, too hateful and unjust to just survive. It forcibly alienated the worker from his tools of production and hence his specifically human substance, leaving him vulnerable to exploitation. It sacrificed the "productive life of man," to the "money system," use-value to exchange value. (Skidelsky and Skidelsky, 2012)

This financialization of human effort depletes us of our ability to contribute additional value in regard to innovation and creativity. To be known as an employee number and a cost on a spreadsheet dehumanizes us from our potential to do more than the number we have been allocated. Economists may try to convince us that it is possible to measure something only in financial terms. We have been taught that we can manage only what gets measured and something that can be given a number is something that can be verified. But we have learnt through the credit crunch that what the numbers say isn't always true and is not representative of the reality of a situation. It might be that the full value of an individual may be difficult to measure, but potential and engagement does have a return on investment, and it does impact the bottom line. Humanity is more profound than purely our economic efforts and the return on capital employed. As the West has shifted from a manufacturing to a knowledge industry, it has become increasingly difficult to measure the productivity and worth of each individual. What value you put on knowledge and the outputs it produces are far more subjective than the production of a tangible object. In education we are measured by examinations and in work we are, in most instances, measured by competencies. But our true value lies not in what we do, but in who we are. Many organizations decry the lack of innovation and creativity, while at the same time creating processes, systems, and an organizational environment where creativity is stifled in the grip of quarterly financial reporting, managerialism, and process efficiency.

When an organization is faced with cost cutting due to economic pressures, leadership teams and accountants scour the ledgers to see where there can be a reduction in cost, and they come to rest at the cost of human capital. A simple calculation is made as to what cost needs to be trimmed and the conversation moves on to other cost savings: marketing budgets, training budgets, capital equipment, stock holding, etc. But the numbers that accountants look at are a cost number not a value number. It can't place a measure on how the group dynamics create a chemistry that sparks ideas and creativity, or how a seemingly unimportant person can be the catalyst for innovation or performance. Too often, after a spate of redundancies, organizations come to the crushing realization that they have just let go someone who help the key to an important piece of knowledge vital to the organization. Human beings aren't capital that can be boxed or reduced to a simple or singular dimension.

In delayering exercises, managers are instructed as to what their new revised budget for headcount is and told to get on with it. The managers then pull together a restructure plan to decide how to reduce headcount while still getting the same work done without any detriment to customer service and quality, and a redundancy program begins. The result is that an individual's life will be turned upside down. But what has been lost from the organization is greater than the value of a job being done. It is the reason why organizations now take great pains over recruitment and selection. It is no longer enough to have bums on seats, but to have someone who has the right attitude, behavior, knowledge, skills, and the X-factor that ensures that more than a task is completed. It is the reason why, despite the advances in robotics, many jobs are still done by human beings. The ability to contribute greater than the sum of our parts, especially when we are placed in an environment where group dynamics and culture enhance our talents, means that human beings will always be more than a number. Our potential is far greater than our performance, our discretionary effort far greater than the task in hand. But of course we can't measure potential or possible discretionary effort. If a manager was asked to give a value of their capital equipment—then they could tell you the cost and the benefit associated with the plant in their business' what is more, they'll be able to tell you the utilization of the capital equipment, how much of its potential the organization is actually tapping into. So we do value potential, just not that of people.

Temperatism challenges business leaders to adopt a new perspective. It asks organizations not to count what the people are costing, but understand what value they are adding and what value they could add that the organization is not yet providing the opportunity to release. Leaders will find that the organizations profit and loss is missing an important line in assets—people potential value, or PPV for those who like three-letter acronyms. PPV refers to the ability of organizations to achieve the maximum contribution of individual talent potential in order to contribute to the overall effectiveness of the organization's efforts. Motivation theory demonstrates that as individuals are allowed to contribute more fully of themselves to their work and take responsibility for the work that they deliver, they are able to develop their ability to realize their full potential. If you were to question executives as to whether people are their number one priority, their answer will be yes. But question them further and they will eventually admit that people don't come first, profits do. You only have to look at their people practices to realize the true priority of the business. An organization is like a garden, which has great potential for growth and beauty. But cultivating a garden requires resources, time, and effort. It also demands that the organizational leadership look out for and deal with weeds, removing them as necessary to avoid them from growing and killing the plants that have been planted.

Purposeful Endeavor

If an organization fails to grow and change, adapting to the shifts in the environment in which it operates, it will die. But being able to change and adapt requires an organization to understand what it is in the first place, what its start point is; a pursuit of growth and profit without end does not engage the character of employees. Why an organization exists provides the foundation stone upon which it can create structures and processes for its employees to build their capability to deliver organizational strategy. Like a building without a solid, firm, and unshakeable foundation, an organization without purpose is unlikely to survive in the long term. The fact is that all organizations have a purpose, even if it has got lost along the way. Organizational purpose tends to happen at the point at which the founder decides there is a reason to create the organization in the first place. Organizations don't just exist to make money or profit for their shareholders; they exist for a higher purpose.

It is the leader's job to do the work that the organization is designed to do. Not keeping busy, not squeezing square pegs into round holes, but expending time, energy, and resource on achieving the organization-shaped purpose. Leaders need to be at the helm, steering the organizational ship to do immeasurably more than they ask or imagine. At the same time individual employees must be released to explore and achieve their talent potential so that they contribute not just to the task at hand but a higher value that satisfies not just the organizational purpose but the very core of self. Rather than self-interest, the pursuit of self-fulfillment is a higher placed purpose.

Human beings, even the most rational and logical of us, are better at focusing on something we can feel a connection to. For the vast majority of us, we cannot feel a connection to a million or billion pound number, because we have no experience of what that means; it is meaningless. In Shaping the Future research, the CIPD found that

> feelings towards profit-related purpose are generally negative, with employees saying it makes them feel de-motivated and less

committed to their organisation. Nonetheless, just under a third feel that focusing on investors is the right thing to do in the long run. It seems in order to produce a motivated and committed workforce, the main purpose needs to have a social basis to it— profit does not seem to "kick start" the workforce. (CIPD, 2010)

The problem with profit as the core reason for an organization's existence is that the majority of employees in an organization struggle to connect what they do on a day-to-day basis with a number. The problem with profit as a purpose is that the majority of employees in an organization don't care about a number. They may care when it comes to paying their bonus if it is linked to the profit number. But individual employees in a firm cannot connect what they do on a day-to-day basis with profit. For people to commit to the direction an organization is taking, they require an organization to have a meaningful purpose. Although strategic planning focuses the business leader on how to deliver an organization's strategy, it fails to explain where strategy is created. In a modern global economy, organizational purpose is at the heart of the organization and must articulate not what must be done, but why we are here.

So if not a profit-focused purpose, then what? There are many types of purpose that an organization can have, but purpose broadly falls into two categories. The first is a societal purpose, which focuses on the contribution that the organization makes to society as a whole, such as being fair or acting with respect. The second category of purpose is one that defines human endeavor in terms of a business challenge such as quality or recognition as the best. Organizational purpose inspires purposefulness in employees and that should be something all organizations aspire to. In the development practitioner world there is a much used story about a NASA employee who was sweeping the floor and was asked by John F. Kennedy what his job was; he answered it was to put a man on the moon, a purpose that was articulated by Kennedy in 1969. But this story illustrates the power of purpose more than any other. The individual had purpose in what he was doing, he was putting a man on the moon. Imagine the pride that the employee must have put into his job and how motivated he must have felt when his alarm clock rang in the morning. The idea of aligning a diverse employee population, who all have different ideas, values, and beliefs, to one goal can from the outset seem a daunting task. Take that to a local level, national level, or global level, and the likelihood of everyone heading in the same direction diminishes with every individual who comes on board.

Very often organizations and societies are defeated in their purposes because of an inability to come together and find agreement on how to move forward. The conflict in the Middle East demonstrates the difficultly of alignment even when the goal of peace is held by all sides. The problems of alignment begin very simply when one individual or group chooses to make self-interested decisions and choose to present data and information in a manner that is beneficial to their interest rather than the common purpose. Different attitudes toward appropriate behavior, transparency, and fear of losing face or positions of power all play a part in tearing apart talks and finding common ground. Self-serving behavior can be limited by expectations. The belief that compromise should be reciprocal and the expectation that if one party takes a step or makes a decision that helps another toward preserving their interests should be rewarded with like behavior.

Reciprocity therefore oils the wheels of conflict resolution. Often though it is these first tentative steps that are the most difficult to make and if reciprocal behavior does not happen it leads to greater conflict and withdrawal of cooperation. The U.S. Debt Crisis in July 2011 was extraordinarily ordinary. It's extraordinary because the parties involved were putting the future of their whole country in crisis for the sake of politics, self-interest, and personal point scoring. It's ordinary because it happens all the time where strong beliefs are involved. The issues that the politicians were grappling with were actually nothing to do with the debt crisis, but rather the fact that their normal relationship is based on conflict rather than collaboration. Differences of opinion regarding what the right thing to do next became less about doing the right thing and more about personal point scoring than about solving the problem at hand. Purpose had got lost in the midst of politicking.

The situation in the United States did highlight the requirement for different thinking and the importance of alignment especially in a crisis. Collaboration becomes more difficult to nurture in a crisis because strong ideas and opinions become more entrenched. Therefore, alignment and reciprocity need to be nurtured as part of the day job; they need to be ordinary rather than extraordinary. If parties have demonstrated that they can be trusted to work together for the common interest and deliver on promises when things are calm, then in a crisis the "trust bank" holds real value in getting things done. If the trust bank is empty because of a history of pursuing individual self-interest, as demonstrated by the financial institutions even in the period following the credit crunch and bail-outs, then the process of alignment to a common purpose takes a bigger leap of faith and a demonstration of faith by one party. While both sides think of the other as untrustworthy, alignment is impossible and deeply held opinions and beliefs about the importance of self-interest become immovable and concessions will not be made. While the "me first" mind-set overshadows the needs of the common interest, alignment cannot and will not be made.

The impetuous for the Peace Settlement in Ireland came from the Republicans, who after decades of fighting a system that they fundamentally disagreed with decided instead to play by the rules of the system in order to achieve their aims and ultimately delivered the route of alignment to and delivery of a common purpose. In organizations, the alignment of purpose can take a number of forms. It may be between individuals working on a project, departments and functions working together to deliver an organization-wide solution, being in partnership with customers, or working with competitors to deliver vital solutions in an industry context. Whatever the context, alignment of purpose is the key to the delivery of results and performance. Fighting can be the death knell of the successful completion of a project, and splits and disagreements can lead to the poor implementation of a solution—and are often the cause of the dire success rates of change projects. It is only by laying aside strong opinions, beliefs, and secular self-interested thinking and a steady focus on the common interest or doing good that progress can be made. By asking yourself *what is right for right now,* it is possible to lay aside the past and concentrate on finding a solution, even if, like in the situation Sinn Fein found itself, the process of achieving the common interest goes against some of what you believe. However, it becomes possible when concentrating completely on the here and now, to lay aside previously immovable beliefs.

Defining Purpose

In pursuing a Temperatist agenda, government, society, and organizations must answer the question, what is our purpose? You may think that it might be playing with semantics to talk about purpose. There is so much management speak already, so what is so different about using the word *purpose* as opposed to strategy. The *Oxford English Dictionary* defines purpose as "the reason for which something is done or created or for which something exists" whereas strategy is about a plan of action; at an individual level, purpose is being rather than doing. So when an organization approaches the question "What is our purpose?" the answer is not a profit number, or a growth percentage; for society purpose is not a GDP figure. Rather purpose is what is at the very heart of why we exist. When all is said and done, it is what really matters.

Purpose is a central feature of Temperatism. "Who are you?" and "Why are you here?" are the first questions that should be explored in regard to individuals. In regard to an organization, "What is the organization's purpose?" Neither strategy nor financial targets, are the start point of any organizational endeavor and importantly what purpose is there for the profit and wealth created by the organization. For societies, "What is the purpose of society?" needs to be explored and understood, in regard to both the social structures used to create cohesion and the culture and the type of social values we wish to live by. Why are the questions so important to Temperatism, whether at an individual, organizational, political, social, or human level? Because who we are drives all our actions and behaviors, it gives us the motivation to do something, or not, and is distinct as our fingerprints and DNA. Why we are here is the food that gives us the energy to keep going regardless of obstacles and difficulties. It is more than a goal that once reached can be checked off our to-do list, but rather a dynamic purpose that not only changes us and our actions, but has the power to make a difference to those around us.

Is it possible for an organization or society to be successful without having clarity around its purpose? Yes. Organizations and societies have been and will continue to be successful without having a purpose. The question is not of success, but sustainability of the success achieved. The world is changing and the pace of change is increasing. The issue and challenge is how a Temperatist agenda convinces government and organizations that the market system based on quarterly reporting is flawed and that a purpose-driven agenda, based on doing good, will not only replicate financial success but also create long-term sustainability that benefits investors and the society. It would be difficult to find a mechanism that can be utilized to demonstrate to an organization that produces consistently good financial results, that they are measuring the wrong thing, and that their performance may not be as good as they believe it to be. The challenge is to redefine competitive advantage, to shift success measures from efficiency to effectiveness, and measure organizational success on the impact it has as a part of the whole, rather than in splendid isolation.

Today organizations marvel in the creation of efficiency. Efficiency can be repeated, copied, and adapted and is based on structures, processes, and hard systems. Effectiveness comes from utilizing knowledge, innovation, and creativity, which comes from people. People are unique and provide a critical element of sustainability in regard to success. Efficiency can be created without meaning being understood; it can be achieved by doing things better. But effectiveness requires people to have a sense of purpose and for people to commit to the direction that is being taken, people require a meaningful purpose. Therefore, in the new global economy, the difference between being able to sustain performance or not will be the clarity of purpose, which is shared among all individuals involved in the endeavor. Purpose connects the talent of individuals within society or the organization with the activities that take place. Understanding the connection between the people, the talent they possess, and the talent required for the achievement of purpose to be achieved creates the environment in which the individual's potential can be released. Creating an individual's role around the talents they possess and aligning the talent to the needs of the organization's purpose provides the foundation for mapping the talent required, while enabling individuals to develop a self-awareness of how their talent can be used and how they can develop their capability in line with the needs of the efforts toward achieving purpose. If individuals are unable to express their talent in their day-to-day activity, purpose cannot be sustained or achieved. It is the ability of individuals to express their potential flowing into the purpose that helps engender an environment for sustainable performance. Without people using their talent, purpose cannot be expressed or achieved. With talent being released to achieve its full potential, the achievement of purpose becomes possible. The talent within breathes life into purpose and creates the pathways by which activities have the momentum to move society or organizations forward.

Purpose also provides the glue by which individuals connect and group together. It provides the focus for relationship building and collaboration between individuals, teams, and groups collectively helping the pursuit of purpose. Harmonious communities tap into the collective talent gathered from around the wider network, making it is possible for performance to expand from pockets to an organization or society, wide sharing of expertise, knowledge, skill, and experience. Harmonious communities therefore enable purpose to become meaningful, shared, and translated into activity. Take for example the architects of the abolition of the slave trade, William Wilberforce. His purpose had implications beyond purely that of stopping the trade in human suffering. The following extract from UCB Word from today is a brilliant example of the impact and ramifications of a purpose-driven life.

> Wilberforce presided over a social earthquake that rearranged the continents and whose magnitude we are only now beginning to fully appreciate. During his first years in Parliament, Wilberforce wined and dined each night and was touted as "the wittiest man in all of England." Looking back on it he wrote, "For the first years I was in Parliament I did nothing—nothing of any purpose." But in committing to Christ he discovered his life's purpose. It was not about achieving personal greatness, but about serving others. (The UCB, 2012)

Individuals don't have to have a religious conversion to have a purpose in life, but having a purpose is more than simply an individual setting a goal that affects them as an individual. A purpose is always within the context of the setting in which a person lives or an organization in which they operate. How a person lives and what they do with their life will affect those around them, stranger or friend. Our lives do not exist in a vacuum and our actions can have consequences, intended and unintended, that can change the world for better or worse. Many individuals may not consider it is possible to change the world in the same way William Wilberforce did; for a start they may not hold political office and have no access to law makers. But there are many who have power and wealth, who do not change the world and have no consequence beyond the continuation of inequality and the existing structures and systems. Equally in history there are examples of individuals who have no power beyond their ability to bring people together for a common purpose and a passionate belief in the purpose they pursue, who have radically changed the society in which they reside. Many may disregard their ability to influence and persuade, as they may not describe themselves as "witty." But Wilberforce could well have been nothing more than a witty footnote in history had he not discovered his life purpose. Having a purpose is the beginning of making a difference, not just in the life of individuals but possibly in a way that changes continents. Don't underestimate the ability of individuals and organizations to be agents of change. We are all more powerful than you think.

CHAPTER 11

The Chequered History of CSR

It's easy to make a buck. It's a lot tougher to make a difference.

—Tom Brokaw

One of the most telling signs of a system in trouble is when organizations and people start adopting practices that seemingly advocate methods that are contrary to the very system in which it is operating. Corporate social responsibility (CSR) is a theory that suggests that organizations have responsibilities beyond those that are obligated by law, extending the definition of an organization's operations beyond what must be done as required by national legislation. The obligations covered by CSR go beyond the normal financial considerations such as return on investment to shareholders and instead place responsibility for meeting the needs of wider environmental and social stakeholders. In addition, CSR extends the idea of stakeholder beyond those of the shareholder, customer, and supplier into the wider social context, suggesting that the organization ought to consider its impact on the community, the society at large, and the planet. The concept of organizational responsibility therefore falls outside the traditional organizational boundaries into areas of social and environmental impact of operational decisions and actions, with a view to the creation of a sustainable future. Often built as a policy, an organizational code of conduct, or corporate citizenship, the CSR agenda within the organization ensures that the organization operates successfully while avoiding the associated costs to the environment as well as protections in areas such as health and safety, employee care, human rights, and community concerns. Since the 1990s, there has been a growing body of work promoting the importance of the CSR agenda with leading proponents arguing the essential nature of extending the understanding and role of organizational stakeholders.

But CSR is more than providing a more acceptable or a friendly face of capitalism. For economists, CSR is a convenient method by which capitalism can adapt to the pressures for more responsibility within the free market system. The government threatens regulation that the organizations wish to avoid, consumers show support for more "responsible products," and employees are attracted to working in organizations that adopt a socially responsible agenda. But in a system where the rule of law, which is based on contracts, does not protect those that the organization does not have contractual obligation to doesn't necessitate a strict adherence to, or adoption of, a CSR agenda, beyond what is in the organization's own interest. Therefore, those who have a stake in the external costs created by the operations of the organization do not form part of capitalism's obligations and probably remain outside the scope of CSR initiatives that the organization chooses to adopt. The fact that organizations have to produce policies to promote doing good is a sad indictment of the possibilities of the capitalist market system in promoting a broader definition of accountability and delivering on obligations that are moral. It is a wake-up call to say that the capitalist system doesn't work for the betterment of humanity.

The increase in CSR programs and more recently the adoption of corporate accountability programs have been the result not of market forces, or a growing morality among CEOs, but rather of an increased level of activism from pressure groups and consumers. During the 1970s and 1980s there were a series of public scandals, environmental disasters, and human rights abuses perpetrated by big business that exposed Western consumers to the true level of the external costs of the products they were buying. Particular organizations were exposed, as was a growing focus on specific industries, all caught out causing widespread damage to the community in which they were operating. In the wake of appalling breaches of health and safety, chemical and oil spills having a devastating impact on the environment, and illegal activities, organizations began to take note of the impact bad behavior and operational practices were having on their reputation, which in turn impacted the share price. By the 1990s consumer activism shifted from a focus on environmental and health concerns of the previous decades to wider socio-political abuses, such as the use of child labor, poor working conditions, and corruption.

The resulting impact of media exposure and consumer pressure on the bottom line and the occupying reputational damage was great enough to hurt business that no amount of marketing spend or media training could put right. But organizations that were caught in a CSR disaster did not respond out of a moral code of doing the right thing, but rather as a business response to the need to reduce the level and strength of the voices of opposition and activists and the subsequent impact on profit levels. In the first instance this took the mode of increased dialogue, developing voluntary codes of practice, the motive to avoid tougher government regulation that would move significant amounts of *ought to* activities into legal obligations that would add additional cost to operational costs. But the codes had a second and more sinister agenda, to still the voice of the activists and move them from a position of being in the driving seat of the public CSR agenda to gaining control by letting their arguments be heard but restricted to the boardrooms. The arguments shifted from an intrinsic sense of the right thing to do to placing the onus for doing the right thing in the context of a business plan, which had to demonstrate a return on investment. The hope that CSR would bring about self-regulation of moral conduct and corporate citizenship has been successful only in part. Part of the issue is that there has not been a united or credible voice in society to define responsibilities that an organization should voluntarily adopt beyond legislation and regulation. Since the issues that CSR focuses on, such as employee welfare and external social issues, are not core priorities for management, there is little incentive to adopt a proactive approach to socially responsible business decision-making beyond the immediate concerns of the business cycle.

Hierarchy of Corporate Responsibilities

Leisinger in his paper "Capitalism with a Human Face: The UN Global Compact" presented a model of an organization's hierarchy of corporate responsibilities with a continuum, which places corporate philanthropy at the pinnacle of corporate responsibility excellence, through to the *essential* of complying with regulation at the bottom of the hierarchy.

The model outlines the way in which CSR divides into areas of legal compliance, good management practice, and those things considered as optional extras; it is interesting to note that citizenship is based on strategic decision-making, not moral obligations. Leisinger states that "companies . . . add value to society and the national economy by providing products and services that meet customer needs or enhance their quality of life" (Leisinger, 2007). This implies that the focus of CSR is on the organization's operational confines rather than the role of the organization in the context of wider societal needs.

Leisinger's model outlines the essentials of CSR as ensuring that the organization is working within the confines of local, national, and global laws and regulation to ensure that the organization does not act illegally avoiding the consequences of being caught out, in regard to both legal action and the accompanying reputational damage. In the UK, these laws will cover a variety of areas of operation, including equal rights, health and safety, and employment law in relation to human resources, consumer regulations in regard to product and services provided, financial regulation and tax laws to avoid fraudulent activities and environmental legislation. The use of regulation to manage otherwise socially irresponsible actions by organizations demonstrates the difficulty of promoting voluntary CSR while organizations are pursuing a profit agenda. It is interesting to note that the concentration of essentials covered by Lesinger, in regard to good management practices, is focused on protecting the organization from legal action, rather than protecting the society from the action of the organization. Again CSR in this respect is less about the positive contribution that organizations can make, but rather protecting the profit that the organization can generate and the subsequent return on investment to shareholders. Employee wages, training, and benefits are covered in this dimension, but only in regard to employees improving their employability rather than releasing their talent potential or improving equality within society.

The *ought* dimension of Leisinger's Hierarchy of Corporate Responsibilities refers to the actions of organizations that go beyond merely satisfying the legal requirements, but may be expected by social pressure. In the UK, there are an increasing number of organizations that promote their credentials, through signing up to voluntary accreditations; this is demonstrative of the type of actions that fall into the ought category. There is an expectation by consumers that organizations will act responsibly toward the environment, and certification by groups such as the Carbon Trust is promoted as good practice. Investors in People, People Management Standards, Quality Management certification, and Environmental Management certification are regularly cited as requirements for many supply chain operations. Although not legally necessary, many contracts, especially in regard to public sector contracts, require such certification to be in place as an assurance of good management practice. In this respect such practices are part of a strategic decision to support business development. However, there is also an expectation by the public that organizations either will support charitable or community efforts in regard to allowing employees to take part in fundraising during work time or will support a nominated charity. Although these actions may not directly contribute to profits, they do support positive marketing and public relations and help build a positive reputation for the organization. Charities or community programs are usually aligned to promoting and supporting the brand image, and the amount contributed, both in time and in resources, is usually little more than a drop in the ocean in comparison to profit.

The *can* dimension in the Hierarchy of Corporate Responsibilities applies to those actions and activities that an organization takes that could be considered as *nice to have*; that is, they apply to organizations being involved in activities that do not necessarily deliver a direct benefit to the organization, but use the skills, knowledge, and resources of the organization for doing good. Examples Leisinger gives are "pro bono research, community and neighbourhood programmes, volunteerism and donations" (Leisinger 2007). However, it could be argued that for those individuals suffering from poverty, hunger, or preventable diseases or communities that are suffering deprivation, it isn't nice to have clean water, sanitation, healthcare, or education programs, which are considered necessary in other parts of society. When considering the proposed basic goods of Temperatism, health should never be considered as anything other than a must-have for any section of society regardless of nationality, culture, or wealth. Anyone who has survived a life-threatening illness would state that access to healthcare that improved their quality of life and cured their affliction wasn't something that was nice to have, but necessary in regard to their human rights and their humanity. Vaccinating children from curable childhood diseases, or providing advice in regard to sexual health in Africa, for example, should be absolutely necessary in regard to the moral codes and basic humanity.

Self-Interest Supplants Social Interest

The model of Hierarchy of Corporate Responsibilities demonstrates once more that capitalism continues to reject a social argument for a self-interested approach. CSR demands that it is not acceptable to advocate taking action for the sake of doing good, turning many conversations in boardrooms from how the organization could minimize the external costs of their activities to how the CSR agenda could generate profit and a return on investment. Those who advocate CSR within business are not interested in the social or environmental benefit, or the contribution that the organization makes outside of its own profit agenda. Rather the concern is in regard to the benefits that CSR could deliver to the organization's performance. Lean and Six Sigma programs were introduced to reduce waste, because there was a bottom line benefit in doing so. The environmental benefits gave bragging rights to the organization, to increase its reputational kudos, but many of the green projects were already lined up, and analysis shows that a great deal of *green washing* has been going on to pacify those who might seek to interfere in the market. Being green or socially responsible isn't an end in itself, but a useful addendum that businesses use to promote products and services when in fact it is little more than business as usual dressed up in responsible clothing.

CSR has been and continues to be a voluntary program with individuals and organizations choosing to take action in areas they wish to focus on, instead of areas that they really should, morally, be focusing on. CSR provides an alternative to enforcement and government regulation, while failing to provide an aligned and concerted program that can have the impact and drive action that is really game changing, especially in the realm of environmental concerns and poverty alleviation. CSR continues to position management as benevolent do-gooders, seeking guidance and help from interested parties, to enable the organization to act in a responsible manner for the benefit of communities, society, and the environment while conferring the responsibility for solving the most pressing social and environmental issues onto government and society as a whole. Being seen to act redirects the ire of activists rather than directly addressing the question of the obligation of the organization to have a positive impact in regard to the true cost of their activities on the wider social and environmental community in which they operate.

Capitalism was not so much tamed by the CSR agenda, but rather given a facelift. The very actions and the resulting outcomes that had incited activists to action in the early 1970s reduced in occurrence and organizations' fixed processes to limit shocking events in order to protect valuable brands and remove the taint of being irresponsible. But the CSR agenda has done little to curb the excesses of the capitalist agenda. Abuses continue, even if they are not as obvious. Under the guise of lean manufacturing and business re-engineering, there is an increased reliance on short-term contracts and subcontracting, which has meant that many workers now lack basic working rights and minimum standards in regard to their working conditions.

Big businesses have put greater pressure on their value chain expecting the suppliers to bear the cost of good corporate citizenship, while at the same time exerting greater commercial pressure in regard to pricing. Globalization has exacerbated the issue with outsourcing and relocation of operations to countries that don't practice the same standard of working regulations or legislative protection as that enjoyed by workers in the West. Occasionally organizations are caught out when their supply chain is investigated, but more often than not, the incident is brushed away with a level of deniability because the abuses are occurring lower down the supply chain, rather than in direct management control of the organization. Employee welfare is often considered to be a CSR program for organizations, sometimes occupied by awards such as Great Places to Work. I have to wonder as to why any organization would want to be anything other than a great place to work. We all laugh at the antics of certain organizations because of their ability to both shock and humiliate the sensibilities of those pursuing great customer service, while at the same time demonstrating an ability to turn excellent levels of profitability.

The old adage "treating them mean, keeping them keen" seems to work against all sensibilities of what is right and proper.

But in the twenty-first century it is absurd and abhorrent that organizations believe that it is appropriate to pay people the lowest wage possible often with an unarticulated threat, that there are plenty of people out there looking for work, which keeps people in a place of work where they cannot afford to live, despite working full-time. In workplaces that have begun to resemble a modern-day parody of the Victorian workhouse, the desperate and destitute work in misery alongside each other, imbued with the hopelessness of their position. Society seems to accept and excuse the right of employers to treat employees as little more than cannon fodder. HR wrings its hands, discussing the new psychological contract that seems incredibly one sided and yet frets over the lack of employee commitment, engagement, and the resulting lack of productivity. Reina and Reina (1999) argue that "low trust impedes organizational leaders from achieving objectives. Low trust eats away at the bottom line and the overall health of the organization." The corporate machine owes the worker nothing and in return it expects discretionary effort and loyalty. Instead what is created is a talent embargo, where individuals find that their talent is not being used, or refuse to put their talent and skills to their full use, and organizations devise new systems and processes that dehumanize the workplace and reduce human effort and ingenuity to little more than the odd bright glow.

A historic problem with CSR is in the way that it has often to provide a means to measure success and achieve accountability. With managerialism enforcing a culture of managing only what can be measured, the gap in credible measurement has slowed the impact that CSR policies could have on the way in which organizations operate. However, in the last decade "there has been an increase in social, environmental or sustainability reporting and some advances in terms of strengthening reporting guidelines and methods to overcome the syndrome of 'green glossies' that are more about PR than meaningful disclosure" (Utting, 2008). Examples of social indices include the Domini social index and the Calvert social index. Both provide guidance to institutional investors regarding the CSR performance of organizations based on clear criteria. Other organizations include CSR information in their shareholder reports, and many have adopted the triple bottom line model: People, Planet, Profit. However, the majority of organizations fail to report progress in regard to CSR, and the range of issues that could and should be tackled in regard to external costs to operations leading to inequality or injustice are rarely mentioned or covered either in shareholder reports or in CSR policy documents. Many corporate leaders and their employees would struggle to explain what their CSR policy included, and the rhetoric and fanfare around the introduction of such a policy rarely changes the day-to-day operational practices or decision-making processes within the organization. Organizations very often prioritize CSR activity low down the agenda because of a belief that such initiatives are a waste of valuable capital resource that negates the more important interests of shareholders. However, research demonstrates that markets and society respond positively to those organizations that partake in socially responsible programs, and this in turn delivers benefits that cannot be converted into a simple business case. The creation of goodwill, reputational kudos, and employee engagement offers an intrinsic benefit that is difficult for the bean counters to capture.

Opportunities for a Progressive Agenda

The progress of CSR isn't all doom and gloom. There are some very successful organizations that are creating growth opportunities by ensuring that CSR and sustainability are at the center of their strategy and day-to-day operations. For those organizations that have embraced CSR as a way of doing business and overcome the negative attitudes to doing good in the wider context, business leaders have demonstrated that a focus on doing good can succeed and contribute to growth and competitive advantage. Though many organizations may make the changes initially by reading the signs in regard to where future regulation will come, others have been more proactive in seeking opportunities to creatively adapt their business-as-usual approach to one that goes beyond possible sanctions and regulation.

Organizations that adopt a more positive approach than merely adapting old practices to avoid regulation or consumer backlash have discovered that a new sustainable approach breeds innovation and creativity that is good not only for solving immediate problems but also for developing ideas that are critical to the future of the organization. Rather than seeing the complex problems that exist in the world as something that is someone else's problem, forward-thinking organizations have understood that the environmental agenda, poverty, and social problems that exist are opportunities not only for the organization to make a positive contribution but also for the organization to succeed in doing things differently.

Traditionally the focus of CSR has been on dialogue and participation in activities that placate objections to the operation of business as usual. There are some organizations that have gone further and demonstrated leadership in regard to sustainability and responsibility, but these are the minority rather than the majority. For some CEOs there has been a realization that there is a need to do business differently, that it is not acceptable to pursue a purely profit-based agenda, and that long-term sustainability will be possible only if immediate action is taken in regard to responsibility to the wider society and the environment. For some, the realization that the organization needs to concern itself with longer term solution is still within the realms of guarding future profits, but for others, the idea that responsibility truly does extend beyond the boundaries of the organization has resulted in actions beyond purely a profit motive. What does this tell us? That organizations do have the capacity for doing good and still deliver a profitable return, which means that an organization can continue to operate, deliver shareholder return, and take responsibility for its actions—not because it is forced to, but because it follows a deeper moral code and concern for humanity. It also demonstrates that the market can deliver something other than a capitalist agenda and deliver it successfully. Temperatism isn't just some utopian dream that has no evidence or hope of ever being more than the dreams of tree-hugging lefty hippies. Not only does the capacity for doing good exist and is in operation, but pursuing a different agenda, an agenda for doing good, is profitable.

Holding organizations to account for their actions should not be dismissed as impossible because of the wider failure of CSR to control the agenda, especially in regard to the promotion of inclusion and equality. History demonstrates that reasserting social parameters upon the political and economic landscape is possible, not merely in the form of greater regulation, but in a rebalancing of power relations. In truth the CSR agenda's failure to change the culture of capitalism in the boardrooms develops the argument for a Temperatist economic, political, and social model. Capitalism has been given the chance to voluntarily change, to make good on their promises to be accountable and responsible in their business dealings, has been found wanting. What CSR has provided is a platform from which Temperatism can make its clarion call. Demanding that social and human rights and good stewardship of the environment become the central agenda of organizations is less radical than it was 40 years ago when consumer and pressure group activism began.

Temperatism extends the definition of CSR by challenging the norms of capitalist corporate behavior, from mere social responsibility to that of citizenship, and inverts the Hierarchy of Corporate Responsibility so the nice-to-haves become must-haves. Doing good implies not only environmental and social duties but also a redefining of economic rights beyond simple waste elimination and responsible management practices. Temperatism extends the boundaries of responsibility beyond the organizational walls and demands that organizations devote their operations to a more worthy cause than simply greater levels of profit. Furthermore, Temperatism develops a moral discourse within organizations as to their duty to humanity in relation to the actions that they take. There is an expectation that organizations will act in the interests of the wider context, protecting human rights beyond legal duties and sometimes sacrificing greater levels of short-term profit to find the balance between long-term wealth creation and doing good.

While preventable poverty, disease, and inequality exist, there is a moral obligation for organizations to develop robust codes of conduct beyond mere target setting, to develop guidelines regarding choices that reflect corporate responsibility in a Temperatist setting. Not only should employees be treated with respect to the valuable resource that they are, with benefits and remuneration to reflect it, but organizations must also set themselves a new challenge regarding their responsibilities to society as a whole. While it is right that organizations are profitable in order to continue trading, Temperatism suggests that there is a higher level of rightness, which should ensure that organizations use their position in society to use the wealth created for the betterment of humanity. It is easy to highlight the failings of organizations based on examples of corporate wrongdoing and excess and bemoan the lack of responsibility taken. But just as there are examples of bad organizations, there are many that demonstrate the significant impact an organization can make to society and the environment by choosing to take responsibility. The new thinking Temperatism advocates isn't based upon a belief that organizations are evil; instead it celebrates the unique position that organizations have in our society and suggests that they are the mechanism by which doing good can be achieved.

CHAPTER 12

The Place of Organizations in Society

The five separate fingers are five independent units. Close them and the fist multiplies strength. This is organization.

—James Cash Penney

In the last 30 years something has happened where profit has been placed upon the altar at which we worship and become the only purpose that organizations wish to pursue. Doing well for ourselves and pursuing a bettering of our situation does not make us bad people. But the capitalist pursuit of a profit-first agenda becomes bad when it is distorted and the pursuit of wealth is chosen above doing good.

In the UK, privatization during the 1980s transferred the power and role of government to organizations that are now responsible for the provision of essential services, particularly in the utility sector. These organizations, such as energy, water, transport, and telecommunications companies, cannot claim to be immune from the societal obligations once covered by the government of the day. The services that they provide are costly in terms of infrastructure investment, but more importantly are essential services to the smooth running of modern civilization. Their citizenship role is perhaps greater than their singular economic role as a private corporation. As these organizations have globalized so too have their obligations and responsibilities beyond country borders, and perhaps more so in regard to the contribution they can make to the economic development of third world countries. It is here, where organizations are in the front line of providing services and products that are necessary for social civilization, that we discover the greatest level of convergence between private and public interest, where the face of capitalism must be most aligned to CSR, corporate citizenship, and sustainability.

Failure in the utility sector is divisive and harmful to public health. Power cuts, water shortages, and failure in transport and telecommunications disrupt society and the economy to such a degree that it can, and does, lead to social unrest and public outrage. Organizations in this sector are at the forefront of demonstrating the true identity and place of the organization in our society. The challenge, of course, is how capitalist self-interest can be redirected to align with doing good. Redefining the role of organizations in regard to their accountability to society and humanity in the wider context will create and give a framework to a Temperatist marketplace. At the core of this framework is the concept of sustainability, in regard to not only the environmental impacts of an organizations operations, the creation of the growth needed to alleviate poverty, and the delivery of basic goods in the third world, but also how organizations substitute drivers for consumption with the creation of products and services that contribute to the doing good agenda.

It may be possible to re-orientate Western economies to focus on commercial activities that deliver improvements in areas such as transportation, healthcare, science, art, research, training, and development. Organizations could develop commercial activities, which impact political, cultural, and behavioral changes for the long-term betterment of humanity. Organizations can contribute to the development of basic utilities, such as energy, healthcare, sanitation, and housing that are required in third world countries for the effective delivery of basic goods. But all these changes require a societal shift in economic values. Reshaping purpose in what the wealth created by our endeavors should be used for is one step on the road toward a Temperatist framework, but there also needs to be a redirection of what products and services will provide the greatest return on investment by their very production.

Humans Can't Help but Organize

Organizations are a key player in the Temperatist movement for the very reason that they are inevitable in human society. Organizations are not only more than a convenient social construction to facilitate the means of production, but a scientific reality of the human spirit and probably a universal truth. Stick humans together and we will form cooperatives and organize ourselves. Whether in primitive or advanced forms, we organize. Regardless of politics or a public or private agenda, organizations exist. From the day we are conceived to the day we die, we interact continually with organizations. From the pharmaceutical companies that produce the pregnancy test to confirm our mothers are pregnant to the funeral companies that bury us, our day-to-day lives are surrounded by organizations. Ryan Avent contends that "businesses provide an environment where particular cultures thrive . . . The more complicated technology and the economy become, the more important those cultures are, and the more important the companies themselves become, as a result" (2017). The issue today is not that we organize but that organizations are determined to maintain the status quo, insisting that different adds no value and only pursuing the same course of action will deliver different results. Reform is necessary and organizations must realize that their continuation relies on increasing equality and taking ownership of the obligations that they have toward society.

The UK government mantra of *we are all in this together* applies, and the increasing noise from the consumer and taxpayer in regard to organizations doing their bit, paying their fair share, and addressing the pay gap between CEOs and employees is unlikely to subside. It is perhaps ironic that the primary source of personal income and the purveyor of economic opportunity have become the greatest source of inequality within our society. Arko-Achemfuor and Dzansi (2015) note that "until quite recently, businesses the world over simply focused on profit maximization without really caring about the impact of their activities on society . . . atrocities such as child labor and environmental degradation could easily pass as normal practice." As employees we are placed in a hierarchy of division and graduation of our worth. Regardless of our intrinsic value, we find ourselves placed in an organizational pecking order whereby we are given the status of superior or inferior and where wealth is distributed according to power relations rather than the value that you contribute. Organizations have a huge impact on the society in which they operate and cannot remain in a situation where they insist that their operation is separate from society. Donaldson (1982) proposed "that corporations, like natural persons, have moral and ethical responsibilities" (Blair, 2015). If they continue to operate as if they do not, then the public outrage against organizations will no doubt lead to greater levels of exposure, reputational damage, and unwanted government intervention.

But it is more than the fact that humans organize that makes organizations a key player in the Temperatist ideology. Organizations and entrepreneurs have the capacity to challenge and change society. This is demonstrated time and again by innovative products or services that change the way we perceive things should be done. Whether that is the introduction of domestic appliances that rang the death knell of domestic service as a societal norm to the introduction of digital books and music that we download onto devices. It is in this context that the organizations and their control of the process of production use of knowledge and utilization of skills make an organization's operation a political and social action with all actions reproducing values and beliefs and maintaining societal norms. Organizations are dependent on the environment in which they operate. Social institutions, government policies, legal and regulatory framework, and the culture of the country all contribute to the technological, knowledge, skill, and natural resources available for the organization to use for their operations. In addition, cultural norms impact the willingness of society to contribute to and receive outputs from the organization's operations. The noise that is surrounding capitalism and Western corporatism suggests that there is a growing body of society and government that no longer tolerates the inputs that organizations are demanding or the cost of the outputs that organizations are placing on our world, our communities, or indeed on our individual lives. The domination of the market and the aggressiveness with which it protects its autonomy have begun to replicate the military-led governments that use power and threats to maintain position.

The Problem Is the Solution

It is therefore probably ironic that in a book proposing new thinking about business that Temperatism would promote organizations as the best solution available to deliver the goal of doing good and that the proposal in this book supports a belief that organizations provide the answers to tackling many of the pressing issues that remain in our society. To focus attention on the purveyor of societal destruction as the mechanism by which innovation and creativity will abound may seem flippant at best. However, it is the ability of organizations to solve problems efficiently that makes them an attractive proposition for developing methods by which basic goods can be provided throughout the world. But for that to occur, the leadership demonstrated by those socially responsible organizations that are doing things differently needs to become the rule rather than the exception.

Organizations want to avoid the position of responsibility that regulation and bureaucracy wish to bestow upon them, despite their position of creator and distributor of the wealth in society. Even the words *bureaucracy* and *regulation* have negative connotations, with organizations calling for a removal of red tape that implies they are being tied up and prevented from being able to be effective. Regulation has become a cage that organizations wish to avoid or escape, a limitation on their autonomy and a trap to be avoided at all costs. Many changes that forward-thinking organizations are putting in place today are occurring because they realize that additional regulation is on its way. They are proactively pursuing courses of action to ensure that when regulation comes into place, they will be ahead of the curve and able to deliver to regulatory standards while maintaining their levels of efficiency. Many capitalist thinkers advocate a limited role for government and regulators, espousing a *laissez-faire* doctrine, promoted by Thatcher, of small government leaving the economic engine of society alone to do it, business uninterrupted. Capitalist markets magnify the problem of imperfection because organizations are not forced into a position where they will have to innovate to be efficient and manage the costs of delivering a service or product to a particular standard while simultaneously delivering wealth creation.

The belief that there is no need for government intervention to provide the foundation for doing good, is steeped in decades of muscular entrepreneurialism and the pursuit of self-interest being aligned with public interest. To try and escape the wider responsibilities not just of our individual actions, but also of the actions we take within an organizational setting prevents our ability to act and think humanely. The more rational we pretend our actions are, the more irrational we become in our attempts to hide our humanity and in sociological terms in threatening our very ability to function as social beings. Temperatism isn't an advocate of big government and tough regulation if it interferes with organizations doing what they do best, which is to innovate and deliver. However, after decades of volunteerism it is apparent that greater levels of regulation are needed if organizations are to contribute positively to the doing good agenda, address the external costs created by their operations, and ensure that the wealth created contributes to greater equality in society. For this reason, Temperatism rejects the notion of the "socialization of investment" (Whyman, 2007), or the social ownership of the means of production that, though radical, prompts the question of who would be best suited to manage the investment and means of production on behalf of society. The capitalist markets have demonstrated an ability to increase wealth and deliver a return on capital investment. The problem with capitalism is to whom the wealth is distributed and the proportionality of the wealth distributed. But Temperatism does promote a more active and deliberate role of both civil society and the state in regulation and the radicalization of corporate social responsibility within the boardrooms of organizations. Whether power and wealth redistribution and doing good increases economic efficiency requires a combination of both regulatory intervention and markets and organizations working to make things work better. For Temperatism, regulation is useful only if it helps provide a framework of moral purpose for an organization, increasing the role of the organization as corporate citizen and enabling employees to find and release their full talent potential. This is more deliberate that traditional trade union wage negotiation. Instead, the focus is on recognition of the value that employees represent to an organization and an obligation toward doing good in regard to remuneration and benefits provided.

Developing People Potential

Very often organizations will state that people are their most important asset, but many writers share anecdotes about leaders of a business who nod their heads when discussing how "people are our most important asset" while making decisions that show that people aren't their most important asset. In fact, in many organizations, people only factor as a resource to be used or reduced and leaders are concerned only with the numbers on the spreadsheet. This numerical belittling of human creativity, inventiveness, and a sense of self is at the very heart of the problem with capitalism. Human beings are more than a number and we are greater than the sum total of our skills, knowledge, and experience that can be documented in a performance review meeting. Instead, it is that which can't be measured, our passion, our thinking range, and our talent potential that changes and develops as we interact with the world around us that is the true measure of our value. For a long time, the accepted wisdom was that the reason why inequality exists in society is that individuals lack the skills or knowledge to take advantage of the opportunities available. Organizations complain of the lack of basic skills and knowledge that they need for the jobs available, the blame being laid at the doors of the education system that is "failing" to provide the skills businesses need. However, as training in the UK and the United States is done on a voluntarist basis, the amount of training and support has declined dramatically, especially in regard to those who are joining the workforce, with the majority of training expenditure being focused on future leaders. With a rapidly changing business environment, it is increasingly difficult to predict what skills and knowledge will be valued by organizations and result in employment. The transition of the Western economy from a manufacturing base to a knowledge base demonstrates that it is difficult for the government to be the architect of the training that needs to be provided. Education and training in the twenty-first century have "become a kind of lottery, whose winners and losers are determined, ex post, by the behaviour of the economy" (Galbraith, 2012).

The *war on talent* that was instigated by McKinsey in 1997 has done little to increase the investment that organizations provide in skill and knowledge development. Rather, the result of the talent war has been an increase in executive pay as talent is head hunted and taken from the market. Some organizations attempt to "grow their own" talent, but often find that the talent is poached by organizations who are willing to pay to buy the talent they want. Once again, the monetization of talent has led the economy away from producing to trading. But is the government of the day best placed to say what organizations will need in 10 or 20 years' time, when many organizations themselves struggle with workforce planning in a 12-month planning horizon?

There is a place for public education, in regard to ensuring that basic skills are taught and it is essential that state schools provide an education that is on a par with the private school education, providing equality of opportunity at the early stages of a person's development. An agenda must be developed that goes beyond mere qualification standards and a curriculum based on traditional teaching theory. Doing good becomes a foundation for developing attitudes and behaviors that should be built alongside skills and knowledge capabilities. But more importantly, early education should move away from the testing basis, as experienced in UK classrooms today, where children stop learning just to pass tests and instead develop thinking and learning mind-sets. Teaching our children to question, explore, and be curious is far more important than measuring whether they can pass a test that is put in front of them. Universities have struggled to keep up with a changing world and rather worryingly the real value that they contributed in regard to providing an environment for questioning, and research has been replaced with a production line for qualifications that add little value to the employment opportunities of students or meeting the skill and knowledge requirements that organizations are looking for.

It is organizations that are best placed to provide workplace skills and knowledge development. Not only is learning most likely to be effective if it is practiced, but also organizations can develop relevant and timely learning and development opportunities when they are needed. The modern apprenticeship scheme in the UK has struggled because the very organizations that complain of a lack of, for example, engineering skills, don't want the responsibility or the cost of training and developing their own staff. This oxymoron between what the organization needs and what they are willing to invest in is a continuing theme when it comes to development of employees. Government support in regard to skills development grants is useful in encouraging investment, but organizations should not rely on the taxpayer to fund or provide the resources they require for competitive advantage.

Instead, regulation is required to put learning and development at the center stage, possibly with the development of a percentage of capital employed being dedicated to employee development. Interesting, this idea is not as absurd as it sounds. In April 2017, the UK government began charging organizations with annual pay bills in excess of £3 million a 0.5 percent training levy aimed at boosting productivity and forcing investment in human capital. However, inequality of opportunity for employees in the area of learning and development continues the theme of disparity apparent in the wider capitalist context. Those who have educational qualifications are more likely to receive investment in their personal learning and development than those who have lower levels of educational attainment. Therefore, a focus of taxpayer support should be geared toward the increase in educational standards, skills, and knowledge development and professional development schemes for those who lack or have few qualifications. It may come as a surprise to many that education isn't included in the basic goods proposed by Temperatism, and its absence to the debate so far has been deliberate, because of the author's belief of where personal development falls in regard to the individual and society.

Personal development, in regard to skills and knowledge and education, are directly related to the areas of personality. Talent, as it is commonly accepted in an organizational setting, is restricted to the elite, but Temperatism widens the net of talent to the whole population, linked to our own preference and disposition. To declare everyone as talented goes against the norm, and clearly not everyone is talented in the same way or necessarily possessing a talent that is useful to the organization for which they work. But for each individual our talent is an expression of who we are and yet too often we do not get to use or develop our talent, especially not in the workplace. Organizations today do not invest *in* people. Human resources are predominately treated as a capital resource with no more value than a fleet vehicle or office space, and they are reported as a number with no consideration of what value they truly possess. It is easy to talk about human potential, but neither our education system nor our workplaces are equipped to find what talent means for each individual or to help them to release it.

The individual themselves have a responsibility, which has become abdicated in an era of rights to discover and develop their own talent potential, but it is in organizational life that our true potential is most able to be released. Changes are necessary in early education to help develop thinking individuals who have the awareness of some potential predispositions of talent, but for many of us our talent doesn't become apparent until we are given experience, and this is something organizations can offer and is the reason why it is proposed that education and development should be concentrated in the organizational sphere. Focusing on developing individual strengths, rather than trying to fix weaknesses, is important if talent development is to be taken seriously.

In this area, it may be necessary to switch from a voluntarist to a compulsory commitment for organizations to develop all their employees, not least to ensure that all organizations take their responsibility toward skill and knowledge development seriously. In removing the ability of organizations to choose whether or not they develop their employees, taxpayer support should be given to organizations, because of the acknowledgment of the social value that organizations are adding in giving that support. This partnership between the individual, organization, and society is a cornerstone of skills and educational development, and the role that it plays in the economic wellbeing of a nation.

Taking Responsibility

Organizations talk about ethical business while outsourcing parts of the operation for economic reasons to other organizations that run sweatshops or get involved in abhorrent work practices. This ability to abdicate responsibility for employee practices because of multiple and complex value chains must be addressed if an organization's obligations to employee development are to be realized. On joining an organization, new employees are told about the importance to the organization of developing its people until the economic environment gets too tough and the learning and development budgets get cut as well as employee numbers. The organization should refrain from short-term thinking, but instead take a long-term perspective. Fast capitalism means that even profitable businesses are lambasted because the profit isn't enough in the short term. This thinking and attitude has to change. The focus should be on maintaining a steady level of sustainable performance and organizational effectiveness to ensure the long-term healthy future of the organization. In doing so the organization is able to provide a positive role model to the society at large, by having a culture where doing good is more important than the drive for short-term larger profits. This means investing in employee growth and training and demonstrating a concern for their life outside of work in supporting an organizational culture that promotes work–life balance, family values, flexible working, and wellbeing. Outside of the individual employee, organizations should be a positive influence in the wider community in which they reside. Whether that be through investing in community projects, allowing employees time and resources to invest in the larger community, or simply being a positive part of the community in which the organization resides.

This includes the idea that organizations must ensure that the external costs of their operations are aligned to sustainable business practices. This means that organizations should care about the environmental impact of their business practices and should work toward ensuring that they have a positive not a negative impact on the environment in which they operate. This should include everything from the supply of raw materials, innovation in business processes to reduce environmental impact, or seeking to achieve ever-higher standards in regard to business processes and practices. In the pursuit of their purpose, organizations should act with moral integrity in its dealings with their employees, shareholders, suppliers, and customers. This means paying suppliers on time, or even before time, honoring the spirit of a contract as well as the letter of the contract, treating employees and customers with respect and concern, always going beyond what is expected, and finally not just seeing shareholders as a stream of money, but partners. In all business practices, the organization should seek to act beyond reproach. Policies and practices, health and safety, quality and business dealings should reflect the honor, honesty, and moral standards to which the organization holds itself. Wrongdoing should be rooted out and malpractice dealt with immediately and without trying to cover it up.

What ties all these obligations and responsibilities together is the contribution organizations can make to society as the purveyors of innovation and creativity. The leaders and managers within the organization should work to create an environment where employees are allowed to dream, create, and innovate beyond that which might seem logical and rational. The use of both rational and creative thinking should be encouraged, and individuals should be encouraged to discover and develop their talent in order to release their full potential. Capitalism would have us believe that invention and innovation occur only where there is a self-interested pursuit of personal financial incentives. Research, however, suggests that the opposite is true. The more equal a society, the more creative it is.

> There is a tendency for more patents to be granted per head of population in more equal societies than in less equal ones. Whether this is because talent goes undeveloped or wasted in more unequal societies, or whether hierarchy breed conformity, is anyone's guess. But it does suggest that great equality will not make societies less adaptable. (Wilkinson and Pickett, 2010)

Organizations should not put restrictions on what is possible but rather demand that barriers are broken, new ways of doing things explored, and the pursuit of the impossible made possible used to widen horizons and continuously grow, build, and expand its endeavor. Temperatism argues for a level-headed approach to change and the interaction between the organization and the external environment, curbing the requirement for fast reaction with a more stable and cool appraisal is required. This requires an adaptive and flexible design to organizational and governmental structure and planning, focus on self-control, self-restraint, and responsibility in employment relations and citizenship as opposed to rules and rights and in regard to employees and a talent-liberated rather than talent management approach to human potential. Good management practices are still required if Temperatism is to be successful and efficiency, coupled with effectiveness are still necessary.

The Temperatist marketplace will also require organizations to consider what potential area of growth and innovation are available, scan for trends, manage waste and ensure that resources are used at the right time, for the right things. The difference is that the legal minimum, the things that an organization ought to do is expanded beyond regulation and statute, and become a cultural moral obligation and responsibility for all organizations. The stakeholders of the business extend beyond simply shareholders, employees, customers, and suppliers, widening to include the societal and environmental dimensions as a minimum of acceptable organizational behavior. The very problems that capitalist organizations dismiss as being issues for society and government to deal with, become part of the objective of organizations that will develop systems and processes to ensure they are part of the solution not part of the problem. Continual dialogue and debate will be necessary to ensure sensible and timely solutions are found to help fix both a broken economy and a broken society. There will be many with opinions about what economic, social or environmental problems are, most pressing and only compromise and cooperation between all the dissenting voices can ensure progress can be made and real change can occur.

Temperatism recognizes that organizations need to make a profit in order to continue doing good, provide employment, pay taxes, and pursue a purpose that is worthwhile. It's time organizations stopped pursuing profit and begin to fulfill their true purpose on earth, to be a vehicle for growth and caretakers of the earth's natural resources in a sustainable manner for the good of humanity. Organizations shouldn't need to be told to do the right thing, and it shouldn't be radical to expect organizations to take responsibility for being part of the solution to the challenges that face humanity. It is a sad reality that we need regulation for organizations to act in a way that was morally the right thing to do. Temperatism challenges all players whether political, social, or economic to take their place in being the change required in order to achieve a more equal, more harmonious, and more humane world. Organizations are special because in order to operate successfully they depend upon and cross the divide between the social, economic, and political realms. This places organizations at the heart of a Temperatist society.

CHAPTER 13

Conclusions

Fundamentally, the role of organizations in society is to contribute to social wealth distribution and develop a different agenda for the purpose of profits to increase equality and ensure basic goods become universal. Entrepreneurialism isn't bad if it is aligned to responsibility and delivering an agenda of doing good. Supporting organizations to take their essential role in doing good in society means that their ability to innovate and create to deliver doing good and wealth creation is far more efficient than developing government departments to try and replicate what the market already has the ability to do, adapt, create, and innovate.

In essence, Temperatism adopts a model of cooperativism toward organizations and the market, seeking to restructure the relationship between the organization and the society to achieve a more democratized society where the organizations' primary goal is the mutual benefit to both the owners of the means of production and the delivery of a broader social good. As an ideology this does mean that the dominant power and economic forms of the current capitalist organization will need to be limited, rather than developing state-owned entities. Organizations must be recognized for being social constructions, able to bring together people to invent, innovate, and create, for a specific purpose. The difference being proposed is rather than organizations squeezing their resources dry for the sake of more profit, the focus is on developing a shared purpose. Temperatism is a political, economic, and social choice, which sees organizations as interdependent rather than independent of the society in which they operate. Doing good relies on an open market where organizations must invest in the society within which they operate. Democratic governments must create rules of engagement between the organization and the society, creating rules and regulations on how the organization will operate responsibly, and deliver its obligations in regard to basic goods and doing good. However, Temperatism is more than a process or a system; it is based on the values that protect basic goods and a reclaiming of social morality that readdresses the balance between selfishness and selflessness. Human society needs the passion and desire for change that entrepreneurs and organizations can bring in an organized way. It is not enough to say we should be doing good if we do not have a mechanism with which it can be achieved. We have enough wealth and resources in the world to ensure that everyone, in every country, regardless of social class can have their basic goods fulfilled. The key to releasing this potential to realize the possible is through the innovative productivity of organizations.

Temperatism asks society to focus not on who owns what, whether it is wedded to private capital or state socialism, but to concentrate on what is possible if all people were free to be everything that they were born to be. It encourages the surplus created by human endeavor to not go onto persuading society to consume more, but to seek the betterment of all and release the potential of everyone. It might seem utopian or idealistic, but such a transformation is possible. "What's the most resilient parasite? An idea. A single idea from the human mind can build cities. An idea can transform the world and rewrite all the rules" (Christopher Nolan, via Dom Cobb in the 2010 movie *Inception*).

If organization is important, let's organize in a way that delivers sustainable progress and leads to better not worse economic and social development for everyone. This may require investment from government in regard to supporting research and giving grants to small organizations with ideas for new technologies that are designed for the betterment of society. But whatever the level of state involvement, we need to move away from a situation where politicians tinker around the edges to react to symptoms and resolve to become involved in a deep heart surgery in the way in which our economy is financed, supported, and run. Politics must partner with the social and economic to develop a capacity to think differently and create an environment in which innovative thinking and reform can take place. Although Temperatism continues to advocate the private ownership of the means of production, it encourages new thinking as to possible ways to organize, which removes exploitation and subjugation.

Organizations committed to a different way of doing business have already recognized the importance of improving employee welfare and conditions, contributing positively to the environment through setting goals for decreasing the environmental impact of their operations and addressing human rights abuses. These organizations go beyond the laws and regulations that they are bound by and instead demand a higher standard of corporate social responsibility. This self-restraint and intelligent use of organizational resources has not led to a loss in competitive advantage or profitability; instead doing good has increased profits and sustainability, reduced employee turnover, and led to greater levels of innovation and creativity. The efforts, by the few good men of the organizational world, demonstrate that a Temperatist agenda is possible, efficient, and profitable even in a competitive marketplace where others are playing by different rules. For too long organizations have been worshipping at the temple of Mammon and putting the pursuit of profit above all things. But there is a movement that has begun to question the way organizations are run and query the motives behind an organization's actions. Temperatism demands that doing good for the wider society is more important and that profit no longer be placed first in the list of organizational priorities.

Temperatism is calling time on allowing integrity, morality, honesty, and honor to be ignored if there is money to be made. We can all sit back and bemoan the irresponsibility and corruption of the organizations, but Western society is responsible because we have not demanded better. As an employee, how many times have you sat in a meeting and felt in your gut that the decision being made because it is profitable is wrong? Maybe you are aware of actions by your organization, which have damaged your customers or suppliers, maybe you are aware of lies being told to make more money, or you are privy to information regarding child labor, pollution, manipulation of data, or deliberate price fixing. If you are aware of your organization doing the wrong thing, what are you doing about it? Sticking your head in the sand, taking drugs to help you sleep better at night, ignoring the gnawing at your conscience?

Morals of society change over time, but what is right and what is wrong rarely changes fundamentally. A liberal tradition could be blamed for allowing morals to slip, but liberalism is founded on the principle that you should be free to do what you want as long as you do no harm to others in the process. The scale of morally repugnant acts is alarming. We live in a society that seems to have lost its moral compass or at the very least is choosing to ignore it. Although organizations are to blame for many of the problems, they can also be the solution. Doing good is more than just sticking to the law of the land. Rejecting the pursuit of profit as the deciding factor and only purpose behind the organization's activities is the foundation of good business. It doesn't mean that profit is bad, but it does mean that it shouldn't be the number one driving force of the organization. Instead, organizations should ask themselves *why do we exist,* what is the purpose of the organization's existence, and what can contribute to the wider society. The answers to these questions lead to an exploration of new thinking about business and doing good.

References

Arko-Achemfuor, A. and Dzansi, D. Y. (2015) Business doing well by doing good in the community: The case of Sedikong sa Lerato in South Africa. *Journal of Commerce*. Vol. 7, No. 2, pp. 53–68.

Ashford, R. (2010) Milton Friedman's capitalism and freedom: A binary economic critique. *Journal of Economic Issues*. Vol. 44, No. 2, pp. 533–541.

Banerjee, A. V. and Duflo, E. (2012) *Poor economics barefoot Hedge-fun managers, DIY doctors and the surprising truth about life on less than $1 a day*. London: Penguin Books.

Brunsson, K. (2015) Sustainability in a Society of Organisations. *Journal of Organisational Transformatioin & Social Change*. Vol. 12, No. 1, pp. 5–21.

Carnegie, A. (1906) The Gospel of Wealth. *The North American Review*. Vol. 183, No. 599, pp. 526–537.

CIPD (2011) *Shaping the Future—Sustainable organisational performance; What really makes the difference*. London: CIPD.

CIPD (2012) *A collection of thought pieces—Responsible and sustainable business: HR leading the way*. London: CIPD.

CIPD (2017) *Digital Change Will Transform Society*. Work. Because Business is About People. Issue Eleven. London: CIPD, p. 6.

Clegg, N. (2016) *Politics: Between the extremes*. London: The Bodley Head.

CQ Researcher (2010). *Issues for debate in corporate social responsibilities*. California: SAGE Publications.

Cunningham, P. M. (2004) *Critical Pedagogy and Implications for Human Resource Development*. Advanced in Developing Human Resources; ABI/Inform Global May; 6, 2.

Dorling, D. (2011) *Injustice why social inequality persists*. Bristol: The Policy Press.

Galbraith, J. K. (2012) *Inequality and Instability—A study of the world economy before the great crisis*. New York: Oxford University Press.

Gladwell, M. (2000) *The Tipping Point, How little things can make a big difference*. Little Brown.

Hart, T. (1993) Human Resource Management—Time to exorcize the militant tendency. *Employee Relations*. Vol. 15, No. 3, pp. 29–37.

Holmes, D. (2002) Integral Europe: Fast-capitalism, Multiculturalism, Neo-fascism. Oxford: Princeton University Press.

Hutton, W. *Them and Us. Changing Britain—Why we need a fair society*. London: Abacus, Little, Brown Book Group.

Leisinger, K. M. (2007) *Capitalism with a Human Face The UN Global Compact*, JCC 28 Winter.Greenleaf Publishing Ltd., pp. 113–132.

Mason, P. (2016) *Postcapitalism: A guide to our future*. New York: Macmillan.

Mayer, D. (2007) Corporate Citizenship and Trustworthy Capitalism: Cocreating a More Peaceful Planet. *American Business Law Journal*. Vol. 44, No. 2, pp. 237–286.

Meltzer, A. H. (2012) *Why Capitalism?* New York: Oxford University Press.

Meyer, M. (2015) Positive business: Doing good and doing well. *Business Ethics: A European Review*. Vol. 24, No. S2, pp. 175–197.

Naím, M. (2008) After the Fall What the Lessons of 9/11 could teach the world about the financial crisis. *Foreign Policy*. Vol. 169, pp. 94–95.

Nienhueser, W. (2011) Empirical research on human resource management as a production of ideology. *Management Revue*. Vol. 22, No. 4, pp. 367–393.

Obama, B. (2016) United States Health care reform: Progress to date and next steps. *JAMA*. Vol. 316, No. 5, pp. 525–532.

Reina, D. S. and Reina, M. L., (1999) *Trust & betrayal in the workplace: Building effective relationships in your organization*. Berrett-Koehler Publishers.

Rogoff, K. (2012) Is Modern Capitalism Sustainable? *The International Economy*, pp. 60–61.

Rosenburg, T. (2011) *Join the Club How Peer pressure can transform the world*. London: Icon Books Ltd.

Sachs, I. (2009) Revisiting Development in the Twenty-First Century. *International Journal of Political Economy*. Vol. 38, No. 3, pp. 5–21.

Skidelsky, R. and Skidelsky, E. (2012) *How much is enough? The lover of money and the case for the good life*. London: Allen Lane, Penguin Books Ltd.

Stelzer, I. M. (2004) The corporate scandals and American capitalism. *Public Interest*. Vol. 154, pp. 19–31.

Stokes, P. (2011) *Critical concepts in management and organization studies*. New York: Palgrave Macmillan.

Suciu, A. (2009) The postmodern cultural context-from history to economics. *Economy Transdisciplinarity Cognition*. Vol. 1, p. 284.

Torrington, D. (1993) *How dangerous is human resource management? A reply to Tim Hart*. Employee Relations. Bradford. 15(5), pp. 40, 14 pgs.

The UCB. (2012). *Word for Today*. United Christian Broadcasters.

Ukpere, W. I. and Slabbert, A. D. (2008) Triumphant capitalism and the future of human, social and economic progress in the post-Cold War era. *International Journal of Social Economics*. Vol. 35, No. 6, pp. 417–422.

Utting, P. (2008). The struggle for corporate accountability. *Development and Change*. Vol. 39, No. 6, pp. 959–975.

Veldsman, T. H. (2015) The power of the fish is in the water. *African Journal of Business Ethics*. Vol. 9, No. 1, pp. 63–83.

Watson, H. A. (2004) Liberalism and neo-liberal capitalist globalization: Contradictions of the liberal democratic state. *GeoJournal*. Vol. 60, No. 1, pp. 43–59.

Wells, T. and Graafland, J. (2012) Adam Smith's Bourgeois virtues in competition. *Business Ethics Quarterly*. Vol. 22, No. 2, pp. 319–350.

Whyman, P. B. (2008) The case for the Swedish wage-earner funds: a Post Keynesian solution to the dynamic inefficiency of capitalism through the socialization of investment. *Journal of Post Keynesian Economics*. Vol. 30, No. 2, pp. 227–258.

Wilkinson, R. and Picket, K. (2010) *The spirit level why equality is better for everyone*. London: Penguin Books Ltd.

Websites

BBC (2016) Bosses 'do not deserve bumper pay packets', study finds. 28 December 2016 http://www.bbc.co.uk/news/business-38449264 accessed 1st January 2017.

Department of State (2015) Trafficking in Persons Report July 2015. Department of State, United States of America. https://www.state.gov/documents/organization/245365.pdf accessed 14th April 2017.

International Labour Organisation (2016) Statistics on forced labour, modern slavery and human trafficking. http://www.ilo.org/global/topics/forced-labour/policy-areas/statistics/lang--en/index.htm accessed 14th April 2017.

Joseph Rowntree Foundation (2015) Monitoring poverty and social exclusion 2015. https://www.jrf.org.uk/mpse-2015/work-poverty accessed 16th April 2017.

Joseph Rowntree Foundation (2017) The Homelessness Monitor: England 2017. https://www.jrf.org.uk/report/homelessness-monitor-england-2017 accessed 16th April 2017.

Kentish, B. (2016) Finland to begin paying basic income to unemployed citizens. 23 December 2016. http://www.independent.co.uk/news/world/europe/finland-universal-basic-income-ubi-citizens-560-euros-monthly-job-poverty-unemployment-a7492911.html accessed 1st January 2017.

Land Registry (2017) UK House Price Index. http://landregistry.data.gov.uk/app/ukhpi accessed 17th April 2017.

Monboit, G. (2016) Neoliberalism – the ideology at the root of all our problems. *The Guardian*. 15 April 2016. https://www.theguardian.com/books/2016/apr/15/neoliberalism-ideology-problem-george-monbiot accessed 1st January 2017.

Orr, D. (2012) Valuing only work that generates profit is not just wrong, it's inhuman. guardian.co.uk 27 April 2012. http://www.guardian.co.uk/

commentisfree/2012/apr/27/deborah-orr-only-profitable-work?INTCMP
=SRCH accessed 10th May 2012.

Oxfam. (2016) An economy for the 1%: How privilege and power in the economy drive extreme inequality and how this can be stopped. http://www
.oxfam.org.uk/media-centre/press-releases/2016/01/62-people-own-same
-as-half-world-says-oxfam-inequality-report-davos-world-economic-forum
accessed 27th February 2017.

Payscale (2017) Average Salary for State: Wales: Wrexham. http://www.payscale
.com/research/UK/State=Wales%3A_Wrexham/Salary#by_City accessed 17th
April 2017.

Rightmove (2017) House Prices in London. http://www.rightmove.co.uk/house
-prices-in-London.html accessed 17th April 2017.

Vivan, D., Winterbotham, M., Shury, J., James, A. S., Hewitt, J. H., Tweddle,
M., and Downing, C. (2016) The UK Commission's Employer Skills Survey
2015: UK Results. IFF Research. https://www.gov.uk/government/uploads
/system/uploads/attachment_data/file/525444/UKCESS_2015_Report
_for_web__May_.pdf accessed 14th April 2017.

Zoopla (2017) Property for Sale near Rhosddu Road, Wrexham LL 11, http://www
.zoopla.co.uk/for-sale/property/wrexham/rhosddu-road/ accessed 17th April
2017.

Index

OTHER TITLES IN THE HUMAN RESOURCE MANAGEMENT AND ORGANIZATIONAL BEHAVIOR COLLECTION

- *The Challenge to Be and Not to Do: How to Manage Your Career and Maximize Your Potential* by Carrie Foster
- *Slow Down to Speed Up: Lead, Succeed, and Thrive in a 24/7 World* by Liz Bywater
- *The Illusion of Inclusion: Global Inclusion, Unconscious Bias, and the Bottom Line* by Helen Turnbull
- *On All Cylinders: The Entrepreneur's Handbook* by Ron Robinson
- *Employee LEAPS: Leveraging Engagement by Applying Positive Strategies* by Kevin E. Phillips
- *Making Human Resource Technology Decisions: A Strategic Perspective* by Janet H. Marler and Sandra L. Fisher
- *Feet to the Fire: How to Exemplify And Create The Accountability That CreatesGreat Companies* by Lorraine A. Moore
- *HR Analytics and Innovations in Workforce Planning* by Tony Miller
- *Deconstructing Management Maxims, Volume I: A Critical Examination of Conventional Business Wisdom* by Kevin Wayne
- *Deconstructing Management Maxims, Volume II: A Critical Examination of Conventional Business Wisdom* by Kevin Wayne
- *The Real Me: Find and Express Your Authentic Self* by Mark Eyre
- *Across the Spectrum: What Color Are You?* by Stephen Elkins-Jarrett
- *Life of a Lifetime: Inspiration for Creating Your Extraordinary Life* by Christoph Spiessens
- *The Facilitative Leader: Managing Performance Without Controlling People* by Steve Reilly
- *The Human Resource Professional's Guide to Change Management: Practical Tools and Techniques to Enact Meaningful and Lasting Organizational Change* by Melanie J. Peacock
- *Tough Calls: How to Move Beyond Indecision and Good Intentions* by Linda D. Henman

Announcing the Business Expert Press Digital Library

Concise e-books business students need for classroom and research

This book can also be purchased in an e-book collection by your library as

- *a one-time purchase,*
- *that is owned forever,*
- *allows for simultaneous readers,*
- *has no restrictions on printing, and*
- *can be downloaded as PDFs from within the library community.*

Our digital library collections are a great solution to beat the rising cost of textbooks. E-books can be loaded into their course management systems or onto students' e-book readers. The **Business Expert Press** digital libraries are very affordable, with no obligation to buy in future years. For more information, please visit **www.businessexpertpress.com/librarians**. To set up a trial in the United States, please email **sales@businessexpertpress.com**.

www.ingramcontent.com/pod-product-compliance
Lightning Source LLC
Chambersburg PA
CBHW072352200326
41519CB00015B/3739